POCKET GUIDE TO

CELTIC
SPIRITUALITY

SIRONA KNIGHT

THE CROSSING PRESS
FREEDOM, CALIFORNIA

*Dedicated to the Goddesses and Gods of the Tuatha,
and to Michael and Skylor for their eternal love,
light, and laughter.*

Copyright © 1998 by Sirona Knight
Cover design by Tara M. Eoff
Printed in the U.S.A.

For information on bulk purchases or group discounts for this and
other Crossing Press titles, please contact our Special Sales
Manager at 800/777-1048.

Visit our Web site on the Internet: www.crossingpress.com

Library of Congress Cataloging-in-Publication Data

Knight, Sirona, 1955-
     Pocket guide to Celtic spirituality / Sirona Knight.
          p. cm.
     Includes bibliographical references.
     ISBN 0-89594-907-5 (pbk.)
     1. Celt--Religion. 2. Spiritual life I. Title.
BL900.K55   1998
299'.16--dc21   98-5023
                                                        CIP

Contents

The Roots of
Celtic Spirituality

Most of the information on Celtic history and mythology
comes from a combination of Roman and Celtic inscrip-
tions, which makes it difficult to separate one culture from
the other. This information includes commentary by classical scholars and observations by military conquerors, as well
as numerous literary texts written from the seventh century
A.D. to the late medieval period. Historical evidence of
Celtic culture begins with the classical authors of Greece
and Rome, who were strongly prejudiced against the Celts
and lacked objectivity in their writings, primarily because
their countries were at war with the Celts.

The origins of the Celtic people reach far beyond
antiquity, and their legacy is comprised of interwoven stories of history, mythology, and spirituality. For example,
Albion, the ancient name of the British Isles, derives from
the Titan of the same name. In ancient Greek myth, the
twelve Titans ruled the world long before the Olympian
pantheon of Zeus and the classical gods and goddesses. The
Great Earth Mother, Gaea, and the Great Sky Father,
Uranus, were parents of the Titans. Their son Albion was
associated with the Atlas Mountains and the Western
Mediterranean. In Celtic mythology, legend says that all
who are born within the British Isles are daughters and sons
of Albion, regardless of race or creed (see page 19 for more
information on mythology).

HISTORY OF THE CELTS

In the history of the British Isles, wave after wave of different peoples swept down from the European continent and invaded specific regions, as illustrated in Ireland. Before the Celts invaded, Ireland was populated by successive waves of invaders, including the Cessair, who were descendants of Noah; the Partholon from Greece; the Nemed, descendants of Nemed of Scythia; the Fir Bolg from Greece; the Tuatha De Dannan from the northern isles of Greece; and lastly, the sons of Mil Espane from Spain.

The earliest of these invading peoples, the Cessair, were Africans from Egypt. Scholars suggest that Egyptian ideology came into the West and into Druidism through Moses' travels. Other early cultures that had a definite impact on pre-Celtic civilization were the Phoenicians, the Babylonians, and the Chaldeans.

In time, Celtic civilizations spread throughout much of Western Europe, from southern France and part of Spain north into Germany, and then across to Britain and Ireland. In the ninth century B.C., the Celts emerged in waves from the East, though proto-Celtic history goes back at least a millennium or more, most likely to the neolithic megalith builders between 3500 B.C. and 1500 B.C. The original population of the British Isles and continental Gaul was Iberian. The Celtic tribes overran and mingled with the indigenous Iberians, who were physically small and dark-skinned in contrast to the tall, fair Celts.

The Celts populated Gaul, northern Italy, the Iberian Peninsula, Asia Minor, the Balkans, Britain, Wales, Scotland, and Ireland. At the pinnacle of their power, their territory ranged from the British Isles to Turkey.

Historical Timeline

Around 900 B.C.—The early Celts populated the areas between the upper reaches of the Elbe, Danube, and Rhine rivers. The earliest archeological evidence dates from around 700 B.C., (the Halstatt period) at the time when iron was being substituted for bronze in weapons and tools (Bronze Age - 1500 B.C. to 500 B.C.). The Celts then spread into Northern Italy around the sixth century B.C., called the La Tene period. This migration occurred at approximately the same time the Egyptians were first using iron and the Greeks were developing their classical alphabet. It also coincides with the life and spiritual travels of the Greek philosopher and mathematician, Pythagoras.

400 to 300 B.C.—The Celts sacked Rome (initial encounter at Clusium, 390 B.C.) and plundered the Greek Underworld temple of Delphi. This event formed the basis for the stories of the Welsh Underworld called Annwn, and later as the story of the Quest for the Holy Grail. Under many successive leaders, the Celtic territories reached Southwestern Europe (Gaul), Spain, Britain, and Ireland by the third century B.C.

From 280 B.C.—Celts began their first invasions of Alexander the Great's empire, and were known by their Greek name of "The Keltoi," the source of the proper pronunciation of the world Celt, which is always with a hard "K" sound.

Mid-First Century B.C.—The Romans, led by Julius Caesar, conquered the Celts in northern Italy, and soon thereafter conquered Gaul. After Southern England and Wales were taken by the Romans, pure Celtic culture was found only in Ireland, central and northern Scotland, and the remote islands. Because the Romans never invaded Ireland, the Celtic traditions and druidic religion persisted well into the Christian period.

From A.D. 400 to A.D. 500—A Romano-British resurgence occured within Celtic spirituality. Many Celtic and Roman deities were worshipped side-by-side in Britain.

Between A.D. 500 and A.D. 800—Celtic lands see successive waves of invaders from the east led by the Angles, Saxons, and Jutes. Celtic, Roman, and Christian philosophies merged during this period of Anglo-saxon rule. The stories of Arthur emerged from oral tradition based on a legendary king, who lived during the fifth century. Celtic pagan tribes were converted to Christianity.

From A.D. 800 to A.D. 1100—The Danes swept through the countryside. A time of oppressive Eastern Orthodoxy began in A.D. 900, influencing Europe and Britain. In A.D. 1066, William the Conqueror and the Norman Conquest moved through England. Saxons and others were subjugated to Norman French rule, and the Celts dispersed into isolated groups on the Atlantic seaboard.

Between A.D. 1100 and A.D. 1300—Earliest written texts of Celtic literature were recorded. The Courts of Love and Chivalry emerged in France, and the Norman conquest of England gave rise to the Arthurian troubadours and the flowering of romance and love. Chretien de Troyes, a Norman-French court poet, wrote several courtly Arthurian romances around 1160. In 1230, Geoffrey of Monmouth (a Welsh-Breton cleric) wrote "The History of the Kings of Britain," a Celtic-style account based on oral folklore from the Welsh traditions. He also wrote "The Prophecies of Merlin," which include a number of prophetic accounts still being studied by twentieth–century scholars and authors.

During the 12th Century A.D—Celtic myth and legend were recast by the Troubadours and Trouveres, when they spread it throughout the Christian world. Even today, legends of Merlin and Morgan le Fay, and of King Arthur and the Round Table, stir the imagination of humankind.

A.D. 1300 to A.D. 1500—The period known as "The Dark Times" or the Reformation was an era of religious persecution for anyone who was not Catholic. St. Patrick and the Irish Christian church developed a form of Celtic Christianity which greatly influenced Western thought through this period. Between 1469-70 Sir Thomas Mallory, an English knight, wrote *Le Morte D'Arthur* which became the modern standard of the Arthurian legends. In A.D. 1485, the Welsh-descended Tudors ruled, giving England and Wales a semblance of unity and national consciousness. Ireland and Scotland followed a slightly different time scale based on their own past and ancestry. Still seen today, the many political, cultural and spiritual differences between the British, Irish, Scots, and Welsh have yet to be reconciled.

The Fifteenth to the Eighteenth Century—The Renaissance brought printing presses and a greater expansion of the Arthurian legends. This period was also characterized by political and cultural upheavals and mass migrations of Celts and Celtic ideas to the New World.

The Nineteenth Century to the present day—The "New Renaissance" saw Celtic romantic ideals fill the pages of authors such as Sir Walter Scott, William Wordsworth, and Thomas Love Peacock, and the Victorian writers Alfred Lord Tennyson, William Morris, and Matthew Arnold. English artist, poet, and mystic, William Blake, wrote about the majestic and mysterious Albion. William Butler Yeats, Irish poet and dramatist, wrote numerous volumes on Celtic folklore, and was well acquainted with the Faery folklore of the British Isles.

SOCIAL STRUCTURE AND ROLES

Celtic culture is based on the customs and ways of many peoples, with influences from lands as far away as India, Greece, Phoenicia, Egypt, and Siberia. The pagan Celts were an extraordinary mixture of peoples, comprised of both indigenous and migrating tribes, who eventually developed a linguistic and spiritual unity. Although known for their diverse ethnic roots, all Celts spoke dialects of the same language.

Historically, the Celts were tall in stature, with very pale skin. Their long hair was fair, but not naturally so, as they bleached it with lime. Some Celtic men were clean-shaven, others, especially those of high rank, had thick, long, full mustaches. The Celts wore brightly colored clothes, often embroidered, including trousers or skirts and cloaks fastened at the shoulder with a brooch. Their striped and checkered cloaks had a plaid or tartan design designating tribe or clan allegiance, as they do to this day in Scotland.

The basic Celtic social unit was the tribe, or clan, which was, for all practical purposes, an extended family, capable of expansion through marriage, fosterage (as in the case of King Arthur), conquest, assimilation, and so forth. The tribe usually resided in and developed an association with a specific area. Early Celtic tribes bonded closely with the sacred places and geographical features of their tribal locations.

The head of the tribal unit, usually hand-picked by the Druids, was the Queen, King, or Chieftain(ess), who was seen as a direct descendant or at least a representative of the tribal Goddess or God. The right of inheritance and rule was both matrilinear and patrilinear.

The clan name, deities, and animal and plant totems were all unifying forces in Celtic culture. Filled with mystery and magic, the life of the Celt included Shamanism and a connection to the solar and seasonal cycles, as observed in pagan ritual and practice. The Celts believed that the Goddess and God in their many forms and faces could appear in any world, at any time and place, and that humankind could actively enlist the help of these deities. In Celtic culture, women and men were considered equal, and personal sovereignty and free will formed the cornerstones of Celtic philosophy and law. Each individual was important to the whole clan and was encouraged to attain God(dess)hood. The Celts felt that the veil between worlds could be penetrated by any sensitive woman, man, or child. They believed each of us could walk in many worlds at one time.

The hierarchy in Celtic society was straightforward, the ranks being Chieftain, Noble, Landed Freemen and Craftsmen, followed by the general populace, who were bound to specific tribal areas and swore their allegiance to the Noble Lady and Lord. In return for a portion of land to live on, the populace was required to fight in the Nobles' service in cattle raids, tribal disputes, and even in the resistance to the invading Romans and Anglo-Saxons The Scottish clans today retain and echo the tribal allegiance central to early Celtic society.

The Celts mined salt, which gave them certain power and wealth because of its use in food preservation, especially meat. They were builders of roads, highly skilled metal workers (weapons), and well-practiced in animal husbandry and agriculture. The Celts were fierce warriors and renowned horsemen, and Celtic tribes were known for using the chariot in battle. Other characteristics included a fondness for board games, most with spiritual significance, and an intense love of competition and high-risk sports.

Many believe the Celts were one of the strongest and most spiritually advanced peoples of the Western world. They purposely sought the pure reality behind the deceptive and illusive appearance of the "truth." As a people, they favored instinct over reason, relying on the free will and fair play of individuals.

CELTIC WARRIORS

Celtic warriors were feared by the Roman legions, but overall the tribes were poorly organized, and a great deal of infighting over territory, possessions, and lovers occurred. The independent spirit of the Celts, together with the loose structure of the tribes and clans, probably contributed to their ultimate defeat by the Roman legions. The tribes and clans were hard-pressed to continue upholding a united and cooperative front in the face of the Roman invaders, who by contrast were very organized and practiced in military tactics and strategy.

Both Celtic men and women were fierce warriors, notorious for taking the heads of their enemies. They felt the power and essence of a person resided in the head, and the act of beheading ensured their enemy could not return to destroy them in the afterlife or any other dimension. The concept of a single warrior in combat with a single opponent is particularly Celtic; whereas, this ideal of fair play was completely alien to the Romans.

Women and men had the same rights and were otherwise equal in Celtic society. Celtic women were skilled warriors, leading battles or fighting alongside the men. The best known female chieftainess was Boudicca Pennseviges of the Iceni tribe. Often referred to as Queen Boudicca, she was a royal figure of immense stature, a political leader, and a military commander-in-chief. Endowed with divine attributes, she was considered a Goddess by her tribe. The idea and reality of being confronted by these wild and powerful Celtic women in battle must have been horrifying to the patrician Romans.

THE DRUIDS

Before the Roman invasion, Druidism flourished free from outside influence, but afterward, the Druids were slaughtered on sight by Roman soldiers. Roman persecution sent Celtic spirituality and the Druids underground in Britain and Europe. In the Roman-occupied territories of Wales, France, and England, the Celts secretly preserved much of the tradition and many practices through their oral traditions passed from generation to generation.

Through A.D. 700, the Celtic peoples used the sacred Druid alphabet called the "Ogham," invented by Ogma, the god of poetry, eloquence, and speech, who was one of the legendary Tuatha De Dannan. The Druids used the Ogham, runes, and the Greek alphabet, until later these alphabets were replaced with the Latin alphabet as Christianity came to the forefront.

Practices of divination constituted a mainstay of Celtic spirituality, and the Druids acted as the augurs of the people. The Druidic doctrine is basically a meditation on the relationship between humankind and nature, stemming from a sacred relationship with the land and the Goddess.

Some authors suggest that the Druids migrated to the West from the Altai region in Siberia and that they derived much of their mystical heritage from this area, known for its shamans and healers. Other opinions that the Druids stemmed from Abraham of the Israelites or from the

Tibetan lamaseries or even from the legendary Atlantis are certainly more tenuous, but should not be discounted.

Many scholars agree that the Druids probably directly descended from the Phoenicians, most likely through Phoenician sailing expeditions along the trade routes to the Iberian peninsula, Gaul, and Britain. The customs, religion, idols, offices, and dignities of the ancient Britons clearly resemble, and at times are identical to, those of the Phoenicians. One example is the sun god Bel, found in Phoenician and Babylonian folklore as well as in Druid tradition.

Celtic Druidism in Ireland reached its height much earlier than in the rest of the British Isles and Gaul. Accordingly, the British and Gallic Druids derive their teaching and wisdom from the Irish Druids.

The Druids were masters of the invisible, with Merlin the most well-known among their ranks. According to accounts, Merlin acted as a mediator between ordinary reality and the world of spirit, and his position at the king's side formed a special partnership, one in which the Druid, not the king, played the principal role.

In assembly, the Druid always spoke before the king, and often kings were kings only because the Druids decreed it so. Celtic texts also mention that some Druids had small armies of their own and most had a small entourage of bodyguards. Druids, unlike the rest of the populace, were not tied to geographical or tribal locations and allegiances.

The Druids were pagans. They formed the elite Celtic priest(ess)hood, the center of religion and cultural influence. The Druids and Druidesses were administrators, officiators, judges, lawgivers, priests and priestesses, healers, herbalists, astronomers, bards, and oracles for the Celtic peoples. Exempt from taxes and from military service, they were paid in goods such as precious metals, jewels, livestock, and agricultural produce, instead of in gifts of tribal land.

Women were, by right, members of the Druidic class, and held various titles such as Druidess, priestess, magician, prophetess, sorceress, and Dryad. They lived and gathered together in sacred groves and at sacred sites called Nematons. Interestingly, Merlin's two students, Morgan and Vivian, were women who were living symbols of the Sleeping Queens or Priestesses. They are associated with the Faery folk and the very power of the land itself throughout the British countryside.

Druidism is based on working with the energies of the universe, be they earthly, divine, or cosmic. The Milky Way was considered a bridge to the stars. The group of seven stars known as the Pleiades, for instance, were important to the Druids, as the rising and setting of the Pleiades in November and May marked significant annual rituals and celebrations. Other stars of particular importance in the Druid cosmology include Capella, Deneb, Vega, Sirius, and the constellation of Orion.

The Druids embraced the concepts of reincarnation and transmigration. They were master shapeshifters, changing into the animal forms of the raven, wolf, eagle, or deer. Merlin was a master of animals, which meant not that he could control and tame animals, but that he could assume their shapes.

The gift of metamorphosis, or shapeshifting, prevalent in folklore around the world, was a particular shared talent of the Druids. They were able to easily transform their aspect or appearance into that of an animal or another person. Legend tells that ancient Druid Craftmasters used the magic power of *faet fiada* to become invisible (*faet fiada* literally means "the appearance of a wild animal"). In the stories of the Druid hero Tuan mac Cairill, he first appears in the shape of a man, then as an ox, goat, bird, salmon, and he shifts once again into a man by the end of the story.

The Druids believed you could walk in several worlds simultaneously; in other words, what is considered "ordinary" reality is only one of the many realities that a person can experience at a given time. This belief forms a persistent and repetitive Otherworldly theme in Celtic myth and legend and is reflected in their spirituality.

To walk in both worlds, the Druid initiate studied a prescribed body of knowledge. The statutory study period for any acolyte wanting to train for the Druidic priesthood was nineteen years, or one complete "great year" cycle. Druidic colleges and sanctuaries existed, the most famous being Mona at Anglesey in Wales. These sanctuaries and sacred groves were destroyed by the Romans. In A.D. 60, Roman forces attacked and massacred all of the men, women, and children at a vast Druid encampment at Anglesey, destroying sites and artifacts as a means to diminish and eradicate the Druidic influence over the people.

Much Druidic lore has survived in Ireland as the Brehon Law. The Druids were not generally known to sacrifice animals or humans. This rumor was no doubt started by the Romans and the Christians to destroy the Druid's stronghold over the Celtic people. Druidism became synonymous with magic because medieval texts on the continent and in Wales were barred from using the word "Druid." After the Roman conquest and the ensuing wave of Christianity, the words *magus* and *magic* were commonly used in place of the word *druid*.

CELTIC CHRISTIANITY

The Christian Church used several methods to finally convert the Celtic pagan populace. It took over the sacred holidays; hence, Yule became Christmas (even though some say Jesus was born in February), Imbolc became Easter, Samhain became Halloween, and so forth. The pagan Horned God, Kernunnos, became the Christian Devil, and the pagan Triple Goddess became Mary, the virgin (Maid) and the Mother. The Crone aspect of the Goddess was lost to the Christian patriarchy. The Crone was wild, willful, and wise, and hence, a threat to the new patriarchal order. Many of the other pagan deities were transformed into Christian saints. The old sites and temples of worship were seized, and in many cases, Christian churches were built directly over ancient pagan ruins and foundations. The early Church did not always destroy pagan temples, but it destroyed the pagan idols, replacing them with Christian ones.

CELTIC ART

Celtic art reflects the emotional and cultural complexity of its peoples. Entire volumes have been dedicated to Celtic art, and rightly so. The art demonstrates an extraordinarily sophisticated, developed, and elaborate view of the world and cosmos. Part of this view is characterized by a certain ambiguity that reflects polarities and the often nebulous and blurred definitions of life itself.

The ancient beginnings of Celtic art and jewelry date back to the eighth century B.C. and the symbols of the ancient Goddess. Traditionally, the four most popular Celtic symbols in artwork were spirals, crosses, serpents, and dragons. The famous knotwork patterns appeared later around the first century A.D. These symbols, which reflect the spiritual and magical practices of the people, were carved in elaborate detail into stone monuments and used in pottery and tool decoration, jewelry, and all other forms of Celtic art by the tenth century A.D.

Spirals show the flow of energy and the cycles of life. The polarities are shown to spiral inward and outward—as above, so below. Crosses illustrate the energetic crossing or coming together of polarities of energies, such as female and male or light and dark. The cross represents eternal life and serves as a bridge to the higher, or stellar, self, because of its horizontal axis (earthly plane) and vertical axis (stellar world).

Dragons and serpents symbolize the elemental energies of earth, air, fire, and water. Dragons are powerful and wise creatures who carry the secrets of the universe and act as the gatekeepers to other worlds and dimensions. They are the visual representation of the powerful forces within the Earth.

Celtic knotwork symbolizes the continuity and connectedness of the Threefold cycle of birth, life, and death. It depicts a pathway to those seeking ancestral roots and a way to evoke Spirit for inspiration. Not merely a decorative device, Celtic knotwork depicts the weaving, swirling, spiraling, and circling of these patterns of energy, showing the Celtic people's awareness of and affinity for the interwoven energies of the Earth, moon, sun, and stars.

Celtic Folklore and Mythology

CELTIC ORAL TRADITION

Generation after generation, the Celtic people have displayed a great tenacity toward life, fiercely protecting their spirituality, lore, and tradition. In fact, Ireland has the finest body of folklore in the world today because its oral tradition is rich with myth and legend. Oral tradition keeps folklore and mythology alive and evolving.

The professional story-teller, or *shanachie*, persists today in many parts of Ireland, attesting to the Irish people's forbearance and spiritual and cultural strengths. Especially in the dark of winter, stories were, and still are, told for weeks at a time, one part of the story given each night. Several scholars and authors, such as William Butler Yeats, have spent their lives recording and writing down the many versions of these folk stories and faery tales. Yeats believed that very real spiritual and cosmological knowledge was buried within the body of the Irish oral tradition.

Celtic Druids used folklore and mythology to teach young initiates the ways and traditions of the Celts. When teaching students spiritual concepts such as the sacredness of the land, the Druid would tell stories such as the tales of the Tuatha De Dannan, which reinforce and give deeper meaning to the concepts.

This basic method, in which teachers use stories as a vehicle to teach spiritual ideas, is really at the center of any folklore or mythology. Folklore is basically made up of stories and practices that are passed down orally from generation to generation. All the accumulated information and practices of the Celts or any culture is held within the stories that make up the folklore and culture.

Celtic history, folklore, and mythology are intertwined, because the lore and myths offered a way to convey the people's history through generations. Celtic folk tales gave a continuity to Celtic culture and spirituality, with an almost timeless quality, in addition to providing a sense of self-identity. The stories and practices provided each individual with a sense of what it was to be Celtic.

THE ANCIENT MYTHS

The stories of Celtic mythology have their origin in oral tradition, passed on first by elders recounting the tales to the young children around the fire, and later by professional story-tellers, who traveled to cottages and taverns across the countryside telling the ancient tales. Storytelling and ballad singing ran in certain family genealogies for several generations. Today's stories are usually told to entertain, while the ancient Celtic myths and folk tales were told to pass on information, such as genealogical histories and knowledge about the cosmology of the universe.

Teachers passed the ancient myths and stories to students verbatim. The tales were carefully stylized and formalized exercises of the mind. Some students remembered the tales by seeing images or pictures on the wall. Others used such memory triggering devices as mirrors, discs, and shields. Only later, when the stories became part of the storyteller's repertoire, did the intent change from passing on historical and spiritual information to entertaining.

Celtic folklore and mythology has an abundance and variety of stories. Some of these tales are reminiscent of myths from other cultures around the world, for example, the story of the one-eyed God, Balor, and his prophesied death at the hands of his grandson Lugh. Parts of the story echo the Greek myth of Acrisius and Perseus. This similarity between mythologies is partly due to the trading of ideas and goods from culture to culture.

Other tales from Celtic folklore and mythology are uniquely Celtic, part of the ancient myths. Among these are the stories of the Sleepers, which take many forms, from the lore surrounding the Tuatha De Dannan (the Celtic Gods) to the stories of the Sleeper kings and queens, the most renowned being the tales of King Arthur and the Round Table.

The ancient myths are the most powerful and sacred in Celtic spirituality. All other myths derive their foundations from the ancient myths, although the later Roman and Christian influences gave rise to a blending of cultures. Many of the original stories were adapted and changed, moving from the realm of the sacred to that of pure entertainment.

Many actions and belief systems spring from an underlying mythology. What peoples have in common is often revealed in their myth and legend. Myths are stories of humankind's search through history for truth, purpose, and meaning in life—the basis of the spiritual quest.

CYCLES OF CELTIC MYTHOLOGY

The mythology of the Celts is subdivided into various mythological motifs called cycles. The cycles are myths grouped together because of a commonality of people and places; the best example is the Arthurian Cycle, containing legends surrounding King Arthur, Guinevere, and Camelot.

The importance of these cycles of mythology in Celtic spirituality illustrates the close relationship between history and mythology, and between mythology and spirituality. In the first instance, history gives rise to mythology through time as historical figures become mythological characters, particularly in terms of the oral tradition of embellishing the story. As in the case of the Tuatha De Dannan, these historical figures eventually ascend to God(dess)hood while taking on divine qualities. In the spiritual sense, mythology is a way of revering the ancestors and the ancient knowledge passed down from generation to generation.

The Mythological Cycle

This cycle is an accumulation of mythological and historical stories, telling of the five invasions of Ireland, the great mythological battles, and the Goddesses and Gods of the Tuatha De Dannan. In chronological succession the five invasions were:

1. Cessair, granddaughter of Noah
2. Partholan
3. The Nemedians
4. The Tuatha De Dannan
5. The Milesians

The story of Cessair tells that because there was no room in the ark for Cessair, as well as for her father, mother, and husband, she sailed to the uninhabited Western world to escape the flood. But the flood found them, and all were drowned except her husband, Finntain, who survived to tell the story while reportedly living into the sixth century A.D., an elderly man of 5,000 years.

In the story of the Tuatha De Dannan, legend says that the Celtic Goddesses and Gods were the children of the

Mother Goddess Danu and came down from the sky to Ireland in a cloud of mist on May Day morning. These Goddesses and Gods were called the Tuatha De Dannan, meaning the Family of Danu, and with them they brought four treasures: the Stone of Virtue and Destiny, called the Lia Fail or Great Fal; the Sword of Nuada from Gorias; Lugh's Spear of Victory from Finias; and from the mythical city of Murias, Dagda's Cauldron of Rebirth.

The Milesians, who were mortals, invaded the lands of the Celts around 1500 B.C. and drove the Tuatha De Dannan underground. At this point the Celtic God Dagda, a Titanic figure in Irish mythology, assigned each member of the Tuatha De Dannan one of the mounds, or *sidhe*, establishing Otherworld kingdoms beneath the hills of the countryside, within lakes and rivers, indeed within the very body of the land. The Celtic Goddesses and Gods still reside in these mounds, waiting to be awakened by those who summon them. The Gods, together with the Priestess Queens and Sacred Kings, sleep in the caves and hollow hills of the countryside, awaiting the call for their return in a time of need.

The Ulster Cycle

With manuscripts written in the seventh and eighth centuries, the Ulster cycle is the oldest and most famous cycle of Old Irish folklore and mythology. It celebrates the people and culture of the ancient Celts, dating centuries earlier. However, most of the stories take place in the first century B.C., right around the beginning of the Christian era, when Conchobar was king of Ulster. Some of the information suggests Conchobar was the son of Cathbad the Druid and uncle and guardian of the Irish hero Cuchulain, who is the central hero in many of the tales.

The Tain Bo Cuailgne, or The Cattle Raid of Cuailgne, is the longest and most important text of the Ulster cycle. This tale recounts the historical details of the great cattle raid known as the War for the Brown Bull and tells of the hero Cuchulain, who single-handedly defended Ulster against the united provinces of Ireland. The earliest version of this story, reputed to be the oldest epic of ancient Europe, is included in the Book of the Dun Cow, a manuscript compiled in part by a monk of Clonmacnoise before A.D. 1106, who wrote it upon the hide of a dun cow while it was being recited by Fergus Mac Roich. Fergus was a warrior of Old Irish legend in the reign of Conchobar who was summoned from the grave for the purpose of telling the stories contained in the Book of the Dun Cow.

The Arthurian Cycle

Drawn from the life of a British chieftain around the fifth century A.D., the cycle of stories surrounding King Arthur embodies the Celtic spiritual concept of the Sleepers and the sacredness of the land. Accroding to mythology, Arthur was born at Tintagel Castle in Cornwall. After pulling the sword, Albion, from the stone, he became leader of the Round Table. He lived at Caerleon, Wales, with his wife Guanhuyara (Guinevere). After being betrayed by his wife and chief knight, Arthur was mortally wounded at the battle of Camlan and was taken to Avalon by three Faery queens.

Other stories tell how Arthur was borne to the mystical Isle of Avalon to be healed of his wound, where he lies on a golden bed, tended by Morgan le Fay and the "Fortunate Sisters." From this place, he awaits his return in the hour of his people's need. In some stories, Arthur is accompanied by the eighty-one knights of the Round Table, who also await the call for their return.

As in the case of Arthur, the concept of the Sleeper kings and queens is prevalent in Celtic mythology. The Sleeper stories are a variation on the theme that ancestors, as they die, impart their knowledge and energy to the land. Besides King Arthur, who is Welsh, other forms of the Sleeper king concept in Celtic mythology include the Irish Earl Gerald, who sleeps with his warriors in a cavern under the castle of Mullaghmast, and Fionn MacCumal and his warriors called the Fianna who sleep within the land in Argyllshire.

The Fenian or Ossianic Cycle

This collection of mythological tales revolves around the deeds of Fionn MacCumal, his son Oisin, and his grandson Oscar. Fionn was at the height of his fame and splendor during the third century A.D., and the stories were written in manuscripts dating from the twelfth to the seventeenth century. Overall, the flavor of the tales is one of Celtic valor and generosity, and they appear, for the most part, in the form of traditional ballads. These ballads are more common than the stories of the Mythological and Ulster cycles throughout Ireland and Gaelic Scotland.

Besides the stories of Fionn MacCumal and the Fianna, other tales in this cycle tell about Oisin, son of Fionn and the Goddess Sadv in her deer form. In one tale, Oisin meets a woman named Niam, who was riding over the sea from the west on a fast white horse. She professes her love for him and begs him to come with her to Tir na N'Og, the Celtic Otherworld known as the Land of Youth, because no one ages. After initial reluctance to leave Fionn,

Oisin joyfully consents, and he and Niam get up on the white horse, and the two disappear westward facing out to sea. Many years later, Oisin returns to Ireland, and because he has spent his life in Tir na N'Og, he has not aged.

On one hand, this is an ancient version of the Rip Van Winkle motif, but on the other hand, it has an underlying theme of the sacredness of the Earth. This theme is evidenced by the idea that Oisin was son of the deer Goddess, one of the earliest forms of the Goddess. He accompanied Niam to Tir na N'Og, which was one of the Otherworlds created by the Tuatha de Dannan. Later on, much like the Sleepers, he returned, unbridled by the constraints of time.

Merlin's Prophecies

Even into the reign of Queen Elizabeth I, the Welsh gathered in secret on the hills to hear poets recite the prophecies of Merlin and the genealogies of the Welsh princes. Like the quatrains of Nostradamus, the prophecies of Merlin are embedded in cryptic prose with metaphoric meanings. These prophesies, recorded in a sequence of Latin verses written by Geoffrey of Monmouth, include the vision of Goddesses, magical transformations, and a chronological sequence of events that extends into the twenty-first century, and beyond the end of time. Unlike the Christian Bible's book of Revelation, Merlin's prophesies are from much older traditions, embracing the idea of the Goddess who weaves all energies together, unraveling the stars and collapsing the universe back into one.

The lore surrounding Merlin indicates that because his mother was a Goddess and his father human, he was also half-God and half-mortal, like the Greek Hercules. The legend of Merlin stems from a poet, wizard, and prophet who lived around the sixth century, and who, in the Welsh Druid tradition, is known as Myrddin.

The basic story of Myrddin says he went mad at the battle of Ardderyd because of grief at the carnage and thereafter lived in the woods of Celyddon in southern Scotland, subsisting on roots and berries. In one prophecy early in his life, he foretold three different deaths for the same boy; he was later vindicated when the boy fell from a rock, was hanged by his feet from a tree with his head under water, and therefore, drowned. As a seer he reportedly prophesized through odd laughter on three occasions: when an unsuspected queen was lying with a paramour; when a beggar was sitting over a buried treasure; and when a youth buying shoes would never live to wear them.

Probably more than any other mythological figure, Merlin embodies the essence of what it is to be a wizard, a wise man skilled in magic and sorcery. From the most ancient myths into the present, the stories of Merlin continue to capture our imagination and feed the magic of our spirits. In the early Celtic tales, Merlin is first a Druid, then a God. Later he becomes wizard to King Arthur and eventually, a continually evolving archetype in Western society. As an archetype, Merlin becomes an energy we all are able to tap into and use in our spiritual travels and growth, much like the concept of the Sleeper who awakens when needed.

The Mabinogi

The four Welsh stories, or branches, comprising the Mabinogi were written down in the eleventh century. For the most part, they represent the ancient Celtic myths before the influx of Christianity into Celtic culture and spirituality. The stories concern themselves with the exploits and genealogy of the Celtic Goddesses and Gods.

The Mabinogi is particularly useful in tracing family ancestral lines and the relationship of the various Goddesses and Gods to one another. In Celtic spirituality, the four families of Goddess and Gods are called "monads." Students of Celtic spirituality and Druidism usually find they have an affinity with a particular monad. An example of these monadic ties is a family line that includes the all-seeing God Math and his sons, Gwydion and Gobannon, and daughter, Arianrod. Emphasizing the concept of the sacred land, all four monads trace their roots back to the Great Goddess, Danu, who is mother of all things and symbolic of the Earth.

Although other stories have been attached to the collection, the four branches for which the name Mabinogi properly applies are "Pwyll, Prince of Dyfed," "Branwen, daughter of Llyr," "Manawydan son, of Llyr," and "Math , son of Mathonwy." Other stories associated with the Mabinogi are "Lludd and Lleuelys," "Culhwch and Olwen," and "The Tale of Gwion Back and The Tale of Taliesin." The Arthurian romances "The Lady of the Fountain," "Geraint," and "Peredur," along with the stories "The Dream of Rhonabwy" and "The Dream of Maxen Wledig," are also at times included in the Mabinogi (see Further Readings for sources of these stories).

Celtic Gods and Goddesses

THE GODDESS

The concept of the Goddess as the embodiment of the sacred land forms the fundamental roots of Celtic spirituality. The Goddess of Sovereignty, who represents the energies of the elements, often plays a more major role in Celtic mythology than her male counterpart. The Celtic practice of gaining rapport with the Goddess is based on the supposition that by communing and becoming one with the divine wisdom of the land, each person can learn to merge with and release the healing power of the Goddess.

The Goddess embodies and symbolizes the powers of birth, life, and death (rebirth), and as such, the powers of fertility. She is the supreme regulator, and it is she who controls the seasons, the cycles of nature, and the movement of the sun, moon, and all celestial bodies.

The Goddess also offers the promise of wholeness. Her knowledge comes through the heart, and she embodies the feminine power to create, relate, prophesy, embrace, and nurture. Connecting with the Goddess often starts by communing and connecting with nature. Realizing that you are part of the land and of nature and not separate from it is a giant step toward accepting and understanding the feminine wisdom of the Goddess. When you realize the ground you walk upon is actually the Goddess herself, reasons to treat the Earth with respect become obvious.

The Triple Goddess

The Goddess Tradition uses the Threefold One to describe the trinity of energy of the Three Worlds: the Otherworld of our ancestors, the Earth we live upon, and the heavens, the home of the Gods. The All Mother Kerridwen has two faces, one bright and one dark. The Bright One reflects three aspects, as does the Dark One. Because of this, all things whether bright or dark, have a beginning, middle, and end—youth, middle age, and old age; positive, neutral, and negative; birth, life, and death. The Goddess directs all things in this manner: dormant, the greening, and the harvest.

The number three is sacred to the Goddess. The Threefold nature of life plays a pivotal role in Celtic spirituality as the Goddess is worshipped in her three aspects of Maiden, Mother, and Crone (Daughter, Mother, and Grandmother). The Threefold faces of the Goddess link directly to the phases of the moon and to the Wheel of the Year.

The Maiden embodies woman as a virgin whose powers collect and grow stronger. As Mother, she becomes fertile, releasing her stored energies and exchanging energy with her partners and children. The third aspect, that of hag or crone, is a woman who acts as the dissipater of energy. *Hag* stems from the Greek *hagia*, which means holy one. As crone or hag, a woman becomes holy and wise when she no longer sheds the luna-wise blood.

The Goddess Triana is an example of the Triple Goddess and the Threefold One. As Sun-Ana, she is the Maiden, the Daughter Goddess of healing, knowledge, and mental arts. As Earth-Ana, she becomes the Mother Goddess of nature, life, and death. As Moon-Ana, she acts as the Crone Goddess of higher love and wisdom.

THE GOD AND CONSORT

Seeking balance and harmony, the All Mother created a mate, a mirrored reflection of herself. She called him the All Father. Every aspect or quality of the Goddess has a male counterpart referred to as the consort or God.

The Goddess anchored her mate's nature, like her own, to the rotations of the heavens, the seasons and cycles so that after the winter solstice (Yule), their bright natures would begin to awaken, growing stronger and more vital on the Spring Equinox. The bright natures of the Goddess and God rule the season of the greening. With the harvest comes the time for the Goddess's and God's dark natures to rule and roam the land freely, while their bright natures enter dormancy and winter sleep to reawaken in the spring.

Seasonal rituals and celebrations on the High Moons and the Great Days act as the symbolic bodily expression of the ancient love between the Goddess and God. In the Celtic Tradition, the saying "Perfect Love and Perfect Peace" has three meanings. First, it means the perfect love of the Goddess and the perfect peace of the God. Second, it means the perfect love of knowledge and the perfect peace of wisdom. Third, it means the perfect love of all Nature and the perfect peace of being in harmony with all things, whether animate or inanimate.

THE TUATHA DE DANNAN

The Tuatha are the divine race of people in Old Irish mythology who became learned and powerful in the Northern Isles of Greece and the Mediterranean, and who some say may have traveled through Egypt and Asia. They were the descendants of Nemed, who was the son of Agnoman of Scythia. Danu is the Mother of the Tuatha De

Dannan, which means the children, people, or family of the Goddess Danu.

Motivated by their birthright, the Tuatha De Dannan returned to and conquered what is now called Britain. The date of their coming to Ireland, according to the "Book of Invasions," was around the middle of the fifteenth century B.C. They brought their knowledge of magic, Druidism, and the scientific arts with them; they are most likely the race who engineered and built many of the stone circles and observatories throughout Britain. The Tuatha De Dannan deified their learned women and men for their great knowledge, and gave them the name Tuatha De.

The Tuatha De Dannan were depicted in myth and legend as mortal warriors, possessing extraordinary beauty, magic, size, wizardry, and skill. They appeared as a powerful combination of deity, mortal, and spirit. They loved and married human beings; they were immortal yet could be slain and killed; they were infamous shapeshifters; they were invisible or visible at whim and will; and they gave supernatural and divine help to their favorites while sending defeat and death to their enemies.

The Four Treasures of the Tuatha De Dannan

The Tuatha De Dannan brought four magical objects, or talismans, with them to Ireland. These objects, arranged in a clockwise direction, represent the four elements, and the implied balance therein. The Stone of Fal rests in the North Point, and The Invincible Spear of Lugh stands in the East Point. Piercing the South Point is the infallible Sword of Nuada, while the inexhaustible Cauldron of the Dagda, from the mythical city of Murias, sits at the West Point.

It is no wonder one of the Four Treasures, the inexhaustible Cauldron, was the possession of the formidable Great Father, the Dagda. Named for his prowess, the consort owned a great club that killed with one end and revived the dead with the other. In the Battle of Mag Tured, he killed the Fomorians, who are mythologically associated with the forces of nature, such as winter, that challenge humankind. Wherever the Dagda's spear trailed upon the ground, a deep ditch marked the Earth. When the Dagda, Lugh, and Ogmios went into the Fomorian camp to rescue his harper, Dagda saw his harp hanging on the wall, and he invoked it. The harp flew into his hand. He then played the Three Strains—the Strain of Sorrowing, the Strain of Laughter, and the Strain of Sleep. The last strain put the Fomorians into a deep sleep, and the Dagda, with Lugh and Ogmios, left the camp unnoticed and unchallenged.

THE SLEEPERS

The concept of the Sleepers in Celtic mythology originates with the tales of the Tuatha De Dannan. When they were defeated by the invading Milesians, the people of the Tuatha moved into and merged with the hills and mounds of Ireland, which they divided into kingdoms among them. These Otherworld or Underworld kingdoms are known by various names, including Mag Mor (the great plain), Mag Mel (the pleasant plain), Tir na N'Og (the Land of Youth or Land Under Wave), and Annwn (the Underworld). These kingdoms represented the immortal land of music, beautiful women, and ale, without sickness, pain, or death.

When the Tuatha De Dannan merged into the land, they became the Faery, or the "Aes Sidhe" or "Folk of the Mounds," whose spirit and power sleeps within the land, waiting for those who call upon and awaken them.

Traditionally, within Celtic mythology and magic, the Sleepers were the Sacred Kings and Priestess Queens who chose to remain in an altered state in which their consciousnesses were absorbed into the land. Both the Priestess Queens and Sacred Kings concentrated on and worked with one specific tribe, locality, and land. They would actually merge with the land, through trance, meditation, hallucinogenic plants, and dreaming, so as to communicate powers, insights, skills, and energies to others from within the very being, or body, of the land. The idea is that every thought, such as ancestral memories, and action, such as growing crops, is embedded and embodied in the land and can be accessed.

Often this process involved going into the womb of the Goddess—a tunnel, cave, or burial chamber. Ancestral spirits spoke with the Sacred Kings and Priestess Queens, telling them about the mysteries and sacred energies of the land. They learned the connections between the past, present, and future; the nature of time spirals; the secrets of the Underworld.

The concept of Sacred Kingship and Queenship is linked to the Underworld, as the wisdom comes from beneath the Earth, from within the actual land and the planet itself. The Sacred Kings and Priestess Queens conveyed their collective knowledge to their people, often including elements of prophecy, with the intention of expanding the people's understanding of life, their physical environment, and spirituality.

Traditionally, people worked the same basic area of land, meaning that much of their energy was imprinted onto the land where they lived, and when they died, their spirits and flesh became part of that locale. When people wanted to talk to their ancestors for guidance or support, they went out and merged with the trees, streams, and Earth. They released the ancestral energy from its resting place in the land, bridging the past with the future.

In the practice of modern Celtic spirituality, when we tune in to and merge with the land, we awaken the Sleepers and release the ancestral wisdom and power stored within the Earth. The land, which consists of energetic ley lines, harmonics, minerals, flora, and fauna, is like a giant crystal, and like a crystal, it absorbs the energy of anyone or anything that comes into contact with it.

With each passing generation, the residual energy and power sleeping in the earth increases proportionately to the number of those who give their energy to the land. In modern society many of us do not have the traditional affinity with the Earth that our ancestors had, yet we still have a need to connect to and work the land.

SHAPESHIFTING AND TRANSMIGRATION

The tales of Gwion Bach and Taliesin best exemplify the transformational art of shapeshifting and transmigration in Celtic mythology and legend. Kerridwen, the Ninefold Goddess, is a key player in the story of Gwion Bach and the ensuing Magical Chase. She is a magician, one of the Tuatha De Danann, who was learned in the three arts: divination, magic, and enchantment. Goddess of inspiration, knowledge, and transformation, Kerridwen has both a bright and dark face and teaches the lessons of rebirth and reincarnation.

Living on an island in the middle of a woodland lake, the Goddess Kerridwen was mother to two children, a daughter and son, who symbolized the polarities of life, i.e., positivity and negativity emerging from the same source. She had a bright daughter and a dim and dark son, Morfran, who was so ugly he was nicknamed Afagddu, meaning "utter darkness," after the pitch-black night. Kerridwen felt sad in her heart that her son would never be well-received by nobility unless he possessed powers greater than his looks, so she contemplated her arts and discovered a magic potion that would solve her son's problems.

She gathered the Earth's herbs on special days at special times, placed them in her cauldron of water, and then set the cauldron on fire. For a year and a day, Kerridwen brewed a magical potion within her cauldron, her intention being to give it to her dim son, making him bright and beautiful and so full of knowledge and prophecy that he would never want for patronage and respect, love, and admiration. Kerridwen hired a blind man to stir the cauldron and employed the lad that led the man, Gwion Bach, to kindle and tend the fire beneath the cauldron while she kept it full of herbs and water.

As it happened, Kerridwen was asleep at the crucial moment, and young Gwion ingested the three drops of magical fluid, and moved the dark Morfran out of the way. Gwion suddenly gained the ability to hear everything in the world. In an instant he understood the secrets of the past and of the future. Morfran remained ignorant and ugly.

Upon spewing out the three drops, the cauldron broke and gave out a cry, waking the Goddess Kerridwen. She pursued Gwion and finally consumed him: he transformed into a hare and she chased him in the shape of a black greyhound; he dove into the water in the shape of a fish and she rushed after him as an otter; he shapeshifted into a bird, she flew after him as a hawk; he finally descended into a barn and became a grain of wheat, and she transformed into a tufted black hen and swallowed him into her belly. He was then reborn as the sixth century bard, Taliesin, who is considered to be the greatest poet of his language. The following passage from Cad Goddeu in "The Book of Taliesin" provides a further glimpse into shapeshifting, rebirth, and transmigration.

I was in many shapes before I was released:
I was a slender, enchanted sword;
I was raindrops in the air, I was stars' beam;
I was a word in letters, I was a book in origin;
I was lanterns of light for a year and a half;
I was a bridge that stretched over sixty estuaries;
I was a path, I was an eagle, I was a coracle in seas;

The Magical Chase symbolizes the cycle of the seasons, of birth, life, death, and rebirth. Kerridwen gave birth to Taliesin, and hence he inherited her knowledge and wisdom. He, like the Goddess, knew that with death and rebirth come true inspired creation.

THE FOUR TYPES OF DEITIES

There are four different kinds of deities in Celtic Spirituality:

1. Elfin Deities such as Etain, Gobannon, and Mider
2. Monadic Deities such as Danu, Belenus, Morrigan, Triana, and Rhiannon
3. Young Gods called Demi-Gods such as Cordemanon
4. The Gods Incarnate: Goddesses and Gods who have been born as humans so they may perform a specific life task on the Earth

37

The Goddesses and Gods can be seen as both real and mythological figures whose significance is far more than the dimension of their actual historical or romantic existence. The Goddesses and Gods are all interrelated, and it becomes easier to understand their relationships to each other by looking at them as one family, stemming from one source, the Mother Goddess, who is the primal figure.

Danu is the mother monad of all Goddesses and Gods. Bel or Belenus is the first monad to stem from Danu. The Dagda is the second monad, Bridget the third monad, and Llyr the fourth monad to arise. Local deities often embodied solar, lunar, stellar, elemental (earth, air, fire, water), and Otherworldly energies, e.g., the solar Goddess Bridget, the stellar Goddess Arianrhod, and the sea God Llyr. By giving the various forces and energies of nature the name of a Goddess or God, the Celtic people showed their awareness of and relationship to the cosmos. They also identified these forces.

CELTIC GODDESSES AND GODS

Aebh (Aobh)—Goddess of Ireland and wife of Llyr, the sea God.

Aife (Aoife)—A Scottish Queen whose rival was the Amazonian Queen Scathach. Consort of the sea god Manannan. Associated with the alphabet of knowledge, the swan, and crane.

Aine—Irish Earth and Sun Goddess of the Summer Solstice and Midsummer's Eve, with Finn as her consort. Sorceress and Queen of the Faery. Associated with the "red mare," cattle, fertile crops, and wild geese.

Amaethon—Agriculture and harvest God called the "*Harvest King*." Associated with the fruits of the harvest and the sickle, hoe, and plow.

Andraste (Andrasta)—Fertility, war, and death Goddess. Associated with sanctuaries in sacred woods like the one that existed on the Island of Mona (Anglesey).

Angus (Angus Og, Oengus)—Love God associated with youth and courting.

Arawn—Death, war, and ancestral God who was the King of Annwn, the Underworld. Associated with the swine, magical beasts, the ancestral tree, water springs, shapeshifting, and the cauldron.

Arianrhod—Stellar and lunar goddess of time and space, higher love, and wisdom. Daughter of Danu, sister to Gwydion, Gobannon, and Amaethon. Keeper of the "Silver Wheel" or "Silver Disc." Corona Borealis is called Caer Arianrhod (the Northern Crown). States she is a virgin, but when the consort Math tests her, she gives birth to two magical twin sons, Lleu Llaw Gyffes and Dylan Eil Ton. Associated with the silver eight-spoked wheel, the crescent moon, stars, moonbeams, sacred kingship, Threefold Death, and reincarnation.

Artio—Bear Goddess of strength and fertility and protectress of nature. Groundhog Day is an offshoot of Artio's yearly ritual, when the she-bear awakens. The bear chooses her mate.

Badb (Badhbh, Badb Catha)—Goddess of war, inspiration, fury, and wisdom. Known as the Battle Raven, her name meaning "Scald-crow." Sister to Anu, Morrigu, and Mancha. Associated with ravens, crows, and the cauldron.

Banba—Irish Earth Goddess symbolizing the sacred land.

Belenus (Bel, Belanos)—Fire of fire, a God of healing, inspiration, music and truth. Associated with a golden harp, a golden curved sword, a golden spear, and the sun disc.

Belisama—Associated with the rising sun. A young Goddess of fire whose name means "Like unto Flame" and "The Bright and Shining One."

Belisana—Goddess of healing, laughter, and the forests. Associated with the sun's warmth and woodland plants and animals.

Blodenwedd (Blodewedd, Blodeuedd)—The most beautiful and treacherous sun and moon Goddess. Called "White Flower" or "Flowerface." Associated with the white owl, the dawn, primroses, broom, cockle, oak, and meadowsweet.

Boann (Boi, Boanna)—Mother of the herds, river Goddess, and wife of the Dagda. Associated with silver salmon and hazelnuts.

Borvo (Bormo, Bormanus)—Healing God of unseen and concealed truth and inspiration through dreams. Fire of water, the golden God, a Celtic Apollo. Associated with hot springs, a flute, the sun disc, and a golden harp.

Bran (Bron)—God of music and prophecy, protector of bards and poets. Associated with singing, the bard's harp, and the Sacred Head.

Branwen—Called White-Bosomed One and Venus of the Northern Sea, a Welsh Goddess of love whose name means White Raven. Associated with the white crow.

Bridget (Briget, Brede)—Goddess of the Sacred Fire, the sun, hearth, and home. Fire of fire, the bride Goddess of inspiration, poetry, medicine, healing, and smithcraft. Associated with the fire pot, her brass shoe, and the spindle and distaff.

Brigantia—Celtic Briton Goddess of nature and the sun. Associated with the rivers, mountains, and valleys of the countryside.

Camulus—War God who carries a large sword and the enemy's head. Associated with clouds and storms.

Cliodna—Young aspect of the Dark Goddess, her name means "Shapely One." Bird Goddess associated with extraordinary beauty, shapeshifting, apples. Accompanied by three magical birds.

Cordemanon—God of knowledge, ancestry, and travel. Associated with the Great Book of Knowledge, stone circles, and sacred sites.

Coventina—Goddess of the well and the womb of the Earth. Associated with healing springs, sacred wells, childbirth, renewal, and the Earth.

Creiddylad (Creudylad)—Daughter of the Sea god Llyr. A sea Queen, later known as the Welsh goddess Cordelia in Shakespeare's play.

Creidne (Creidhne, Credne)—Master Sword Maker named "The Bronze Worker." Associated with smiths, wrights, metal-working, and craftspersons. Wields a bronze sword.

Dagda—The "Good God" and "Good Hand." Chieftain God of life, death, wisdom, prosperity, abundance, and knowledge. Father to Bridget and Angus Og. Associated with oak trees, the flesh hook, a magical sword, the club, an inexhaustible cauldron, a magical harp, the chalice, and the rods of command. Ruler of the bright half of the year. The King of Feasting, he has power over milk and corn and possesses ever-laden fruit trees and two extraordinary swine, one that is always living and one that is always cooking.

Danu (Dana, Anna, Anu, Don, Donn)—Descended from Nemed, shapeshifter. The Mother Goddess of the Tuatha De Dannan, associated with wisdom and control over all things. Air of air, associated with the staff, abundance, and prosperity. In stellar mythology, the constellation

Cassiopeia honors the Goddess in its name, Llys Don, or Danu's House.

Diancecht—Healing physician to the Gods. Associated with the mortar and pestle.

Dumiatis (Dumeatis)—God of creative thought and teaching. Associated with storytelling, children, teaching tales, the quill pen and ink, writing staves, and the Books of Knowledge.

Dwyn—Known for his manliness, God of love and mischief. A trickster.

Edain (Etain)—Example of transmigration, heroine, Goddess of beauty, grace, and wife of King Mider. One of the "White Ladies" of the Faery, associated with apple blossoms, the Underworld, and a herd of white mares with blue eyes.

Elayne (Elen, Elen Lwyddawg)—Warrior Mother and Leader of the Hosts. Powerful Goddess of Ireland, leadership, and war.

Epona—Shapeshifter, horse, and Earth Goddess worshipped by the ancient Belgae of Northeaster Gaul, depicted holding an apple while seated on a white horse. The only Celtic Goddess included in the Roman pantheon. Nicknamed Regina, her name means Divine Horse as she is the offspring of a mare and a human man. Associated with mares and fertilization by water.

Eriu (Erin)—Earth Goddess of Ireland and Queen of the Tuatha De Dannan. Shapeshifter and Goddess of Sovereignty of the Land. Associated with the power within the land, crows, and creation.

Esus—Aspect of the Dark God. Woodland God associated with hunting, the sword, the Golden Bull (Tarvos), and the bow and arrow.

Fagus—Monadic God of all beech trees.

Fand—Shapeshifter and Faery Queen of Ireland. Daughter of the sea and wife to the sea God Manannan. Ruler of the magical "Land over Wave." Associated with the sea gull.

Findabair—Goddess of Connacht and the Otherworld, of beauty, grace, and love. Daughter of Queen Medb of the Faery, who married a mortal man named Fraech.

Fliodhas—Ancient Goddess of the woodlands. Protector of animals and forests. Associated with woodland springs, green grass, and the doe.

Gabba (Gabis of the Abyss)—Dark queen and crone face of the Dark Mother , her name means Crystal. Associated with the thirteenth moon (Oak Moon) and the Celtic endless weave.

Gobannon (Govannon, Goibniu)—The Divine Smith and God of magic. Associated with metals, forges, blacksmithing tools, and the transforming fire.

Gwalchmei—God of love and music and son of the Goddess Mei. The "Hawk or Falcon of May." Associated with raptors and the fields at hunting times (early morning and late afternoon).

Gwydion—Wizard and Prince of the Powers of Air; master shapeshifter; and God of the arts, eloquence, kindness, and magic. Son of Danu, nephew of Math, and brother of Ameathon, Gobannon, and Arianrhod. Gwydion gave his son Llew his name and his right to bear arms and created Llew's bride for him. One of the twelve that brought the swine to his people. Associated with the harp, healing, and enchantment.

Gwynn ap Nudd—Powerful God of the Otherworld, the death chase, and the Wild Hunt. Associated with the souls of the dead. Always travels with Dormarth, a white hound with red ears.

Hellith—Fire of air, God of the setting sun, and protector of souls of the dead. Associated with a flute that brings peace and tranquillity to all those who hear it and with the disc of the setting sun.

Hertha (Herdda)—Earth Goddess of rebirth and healing. Associated with Spring, the cow and calf, and the milk pail.

Kernunnos—Lord of the animals; God of life, death, wealth, and knowledge; the All Father. Associated with animal horns, antlers, the stag, the bull, three cranes, the rat, a magical serpent belt, and a bag of flowing coins.

Kerridwen (Cerridwyn, Ceridwyn)—The Ninefold One and All Mother. Goddess of knowledge, wisdom, and inspiration. Associated with the cauldron of creation.

Letha—Midsummer harvest Goddess. Associated with the swan and apples.

Llyr (Ler, Lir, Lear, Leer)—Shy sea God of music and king of the oceans. Part man, part fish shapeshifter. Associated with sea mammals, sea serpents, sea gulls, sea shells, and sharks. He plays a harp of silver, pearl, coral, and shell.

Luchta (Lucta, Luchtaine)—Carpenter God and shield maker for the Tuatha De Dannan. God of craftsmen, wrights, and smiths. Associated with the shield.

Lugh (Lug, Lleu [Llew], Llaw Gyffes)—Champion of the Tuatha De Dannan, Sun God, and master of all arts. God of poets, bards, smiths, and war. Powerful sorcerer known for his prowess and generosity. Associated with the setting sun, the moon, the cock, the goat, the turtle, a bag of coins, and a magic sword.

Mabon (Mapon, Maponus)—"The Divine Son" and "The Son of Light," God of sex, love, magic, prophecy, and power. Son of Modron. Associated with the wild chase, youthfulness, playing tricks, the boar, mineral springs, and the lyre.

Sometimes considered the Celtic Christ figure.

Macha—Powerful Irish Queen and threefold sun Goddess of fertility, war, and ritual games. The "Sun Woman" and wife to Nemed and Nuada. Ancestress of the Red Branch, daughter of Ernmas, and granddaughter of Net. Associated with the horse, the raven, and the crow.

Manannan (Manannan ap Llyr, Manannan Mac Llyr)—Master shapeshifter, teacher, God of magic, the sea, and travel. Consort to Rhiannon and son of Llyr. The Land of Promise, an Elysian island, is his home. Gave King Cormac a golden cup that broke when lies were told and became restored when truths were spoken. Associated with the magic wand, a magic spear called the Red Javelin, a magic coracle called the Wave-sweeper, and three magic swords named The Great Fury, The Little Fury, and Retaliator, as well as a mantle and helmet of invisibility, feasting, the pig, and the Faery mounds of Ireland.

Math (Son of Mathonwy)—Seasonal king and Welsh God of magic, wisdom, enchantment, and sorcery. Uncle and teacher to Gwydion, master Druid and teacher. His feet rest in the lap of a virgin during the times between wars. The virgin makes love with Math's nephew, making it necessary to find another virgin to act as Math's source of energy and power. Associated with King Arthur, wealth, and the fabric of life.

Medb (Maeve, Mab)—The Warrior Queen, the Good Faery Queen, and Queen of Connaught. Goddess of Tara and the sovereignty of the land, the most generous of all of her sisters in pledges and bestowing gifts. Runs faster than the quickest horse. Holding her magic spear and shield, she carries animals and birds on her shoulders and arms as she races across the land. Associated with the Irish county of Sligo.

Mei (Mai, Meia)—Mother of Gwalchmei, Earth and Solar Goddess. Associated with green fields and meadows.

Mider (Midir)—The Faery King, God of the Underworld and consort to Etain. Bard and chess player. Associated with the Isle of Man, the Faery hill of Bri Leith, the chess board and game pieces.

Modrona (Modron, Madrona, Matrona)—The Great Mother of Mabon (light). Associated with light, living things, and the All Mother.

Morgana—The Death Mother and the Queen of Death, Goddess of magic, fertility, sexuality, shapeshifting, and war. Daughter of Llyr (the sea) and Anuand (a shapeshifter). Associated with sea shells, cypress trees, the shoreline, ravens, and crows.

Morrigan (Morrigana)—Beautiful and powerful sea Goddess of wisdom and beauty, called the "Great Queen" and "Great Sea Mother." On Samhain, Morrigan takes Dagda, the good God, as her lover. Associated with ocean vegetation, manta rays, whales, sand dollars, and the queen's rod of command.

Morrigu—The Dark Gray Lady and Queen of the Sea, Goddess of life, death, and magic. Protectress of sailors and the shores of Ireland. Has a gentle nature, but destroys if angered. Associated with ocean caves and a harp of silver, shell, and pearl.

Myrddin (Merlin)—Woodland and nature God. Fire of Earth, God of the Earth, sun, laughter, and mirth. A Sky-god of healing and magic. Associated with stones, caves, crystals, herbs, natural mineral deposits, and pure water springs, as well as the wild rose, sweet water springs, the Castle of Glass, and a flute whose music makes you want to dance and laugh.

Nantosuelta—River Goddess of abundance. She holds a dove house on a pole in one hand and carries a baker's paddle. Associated with Sucellos and the dark half of the year.

Nemetona—Great protectress of the sacred Drynemeton, Warrior Goddess of the oak groves, and patron of thermal springs. Associated with the ram and sacred forest sites. She carries a spear made of ash wood with a silver tip.

Nemon (Neman, Nemain)—Daughter of Ernmas and sister to Macha. She is the Goddess of War, whose name means "Venomous One" or "Frenzy." Associated with the crow and the serpent.

Nimue (Niniane, Niviene, Nymenche)—Student and teacher to Merlin, her consort. The Lady of the Lake, maker and keeper of King Arthur's sword, Excalibur. Earth and Water Goddess of lakes and rivers. Associated with underwater caves, swans, swallows, quartz and crystalline formations. She carries a large, bright, white-silver sword in her large, man-like hands.

Nodens—God of dream magic, sleep, and dreams. Associated with initiation and the gateways to the Otherworld.

Nuada (Lludd, Nudd, Lludd Llaw Ercint)—The Good Father, consort to Fea, the war Goddess. Powerful chieftain God of thunder, kingship, rebirth, war, and wealth, who carries one of the Tuatha De Dannan's four treasures, the sword from Findias. On the summer solstice, he loses his hand in battle. A disfigured king cannot rule the Celts, so he has a silver arm made by Diancecht. Associated with thunderstorms and lightning. Carries a magic spear.

Nwyvre—God of space, the stars, ethers, and of the celestial sciences of astronomy and astrology. Consort to Arianrhod. Associated with the nine-pointed star.

Ogmios (Ogma)—Inventor of Ogham writing, very hand-some God of knowledge, civilization, and sexuality. Carries a club or stick carved with runes.

Pryderi—Youthful shapeshifter God, son of the Goddess Rhiannon. Associated with the swine from the Otherworld, the pig and boar.

Pwyll—Prince of Dyfed and King of the Otherworld. A pack of hounds accompanies him.

Rhiannon—Queen Mother, Queen Mare, or the Great Queen, originally called Rigatona. Goddess of knowledge and strength. Associated with apples, horses (especially mares), and three birds.

Robur—Forest King and Monadic tree God of the forests, particularly oaks. Associated with mistletoe, a budding staff of oak, and woodland animals and plants.

Rosemerta—Young aspect of the All Mother, Goddess of abundance and plenty. Wife to Lugh. Associated with gardens, flowers, and the cornucopia flowing with all good things.

Sadv—The Deer Goddess of the forests and nature. Mother to Oisin, the poet. Associated with woodland animals, the doe, and fawn. One of the most ancient Celtic Goddesses.

Sirona—Solar and astral Goddess, Borvo is her consort. Associated with the stars, the celestial skies, and the ancient practice of sky-walking.

Smertullos—The Preserver and Lord of Protection, God of the abyss and the unmanifested. Associated with the snake with a ram's head. Wears a snake belt.

Sucellos—Aspect of the All Father and ruler of the dark half of the year. River God, twin to the Dagda. Shapeshifter and God of fertility and death. Carries a large spear.

Taillte—The Tailltean Games (Irish Olympics) and Teltown were named after her. Irish Earth Goddess who presides over Lughnassad. Foster mother to Lugh. Associated with the Hill of Tara.

Taliesin (Son of Kerridwen)—Poet, prophet and bard. The Hand of the Gods, musician, and magician. Symbolizes the shapeshifting archetypal poet. Associated with transmigration, metamorphosis, the quill, riddles, and the harp.

Taranis—God of thunder, storms, and the seasonal cycle. Associated with the eight-spoked wheel.

Tarvos (Trigaranos)—Born at Coventina's Well, God of vegetation and virility. Associated with the oak, the bull, and three gray cranes.

Tethra—Sea God of magic. Air of water. Associated with the albatross, moonbeams, and flocking seagulls.

Triana—The Triple Goddess—Sun-Ana, Earth-Ana, and Moon-Ana. Goddess of healing, knowledge, mental arts, nature, life, and death, as well as higher love and wisdom. Associated with the golden sun disc, plant life, and the silver crescent moon.

Viviana (Vivian, Vivien)—Life Mother and Goddess of love, birth, life, mothers, childbirth, and children. Her consort is Merlin. Associated with the five-petaled red rose.

Spiritual Teaching
of the Celts

THE SACRED LAND

The roots of Celtic spirituality stem from the sacredness of the land. The Celts were traditionally an agrarian people who viewed the land as not only alive, but also as a great Goddess who provided for all their earthly spiritual needs.

From their reverence toward the Goddess and the land came the Celtic people's desire to work in harmony with the patterns and cycles of nature. These cycles are depicted by the Goddess, who shapeshifts into her many faces, marked and celebrated on each of the Celtic ritual celebrations on the eight Great Days and High Moons. These yearly cycles are organic, sacred, and magical systems of patterns, which require fine-tuning from time to time according to the positions of the sun and the moon.

Sacred oak groves, the ocean, rivers, and lakes were places of powerful transformation valued by the ancient Celts. To them, the land was alive, which meant the very environment and atmosphere sang with energy. This idea of the land being alive is why historically the Celts used key locations within the land—called power centers or sacred sites—to connect with the elements and the cosmos.

Understanding the natural cycles of the Earth, the sky, and the celestial bodies was essential to the Celtic way of life and survival. The Celts had a great kinship with the land; they were very aware of what it could or could not provide for them. Because the Goddess was the embodiment of the land, Celtic tradition is all about tuning into and becoming attuned to the Goddess, which in turn is the land.

THE UNDERWORLD OF THE FAERY

Esoteric and exoteric knowledge were not separate concepts to the Celts. The history and knowledge of the Celtic people were preserved orally in poems, epics, songs, stories, and faery tales. These stories and tales were the keys to ancestral wisdom and the sacred power of the land. Through the knowledge contained in these oral forms, people could invoke deities, learn to use subtle "magical" energies, and work with Faery allies or guardians.

The Faery are the immortal Goddesses and Gods of pagan Ireland, the Tuatha De Dannan who merged with the land. After battling the Formorians, the Good God (the Dagda) divided the hills and mounds of Ireland among his people. They entered the Underworld of the Faery and melded their spirits with the Earth Goddess. The invisible faery paths from one mound (Faery fort, rah, or royalty) to another are straight, and the Celts felt that building on them would bring bad luck.

The Irish word for faery is *sidheog*, a diminutive of the word *shee* as in banshee. The Faery folk are called the *daoine sidhe*, or the Faery people. Faeries are the gentry, famous for their music, feasting, trooping, mystical gifts, whirling winds, and lovemaking. They arise from the hills and mounds on the eves of Beltane, Midsummer, and Samhain to walk among humankind. They sing so sweetly that many a young girl has heard their songs, pined away, and died for love and want of the music. Some faeries are sociable and some are solitary.

One theory suggests the Faery are the angels of the Mother Below, in the Earth. They are definitely not the tiny and mischievous creatures made popular in Victorian days, but large, sometimes gigantic beings that live within the very body of the land. Over thousands of years, many of those with Second Sight have seen and communicated with the Faery, one of the most well-known accounts being that of Reverend Robert Kirk, who was a Gaelic speaker, seventh son, and author of the "Secret Commonwealth of Elves, Fauns, and Fairies," in the late seventeenth century. Tradition states that Reverend Kirk passed physically into the Faery world through the hill at Aberfoyle.

The Faery world mirrors our ordinary world. Whatever is found in one world has a reflection or polar partner in the other. The Celtic people believed that beyond the ordinary world were layer upon layer of conscious beings, such as the Faery, who have no inherent form, but shapeshift at will. In this sense, the Faery are one step away from humankind, normally out of our range of perception. They are considered co-walkers, allies, guardians, and guides.

To journey into the Underworld of the Faery, one must be pure of heart, honest, and steadfast of will, which may be why children more readily see and hear the Faery. Journeying to the Underworld involves intentionally stepping between worlds. This is termed "walking between worlds" or "twinkling"; it involves a physical translation into other realms and, one hopes, the subsequent physical return to ordinary reality. Many stories tell of those who entered into the Faery mounds never to return or only to return several years after they left.

Underworld experiences liberate and unify our energies and perceptions rather than rationalize and separate them. The deeper we reach into the Underworld, the closer we come to the Earth Light. To the Celts, the light within the earth was direct light, that of spirit living within matter.

RECONNECTING TO THE EARTH

Journeying to the Underworld of the Faery is akin to plummeting into the very core of the Goddess, the Earth. This ability and skill is a lost art that needs to be reclaimed in order to balance science with spirit. In the modern world, many people find themselves with little or no time to enjoy recreation outdoors in forests or meadows or by lakes, rivers, or the ocean. This lack of outdoor recreation leads to more alienation and separation from the Earth. In turn, we become more distant and apart from ourselves and our spiritual center. We walk on concrete instead of dirt, grass, or sand. We move in metal steeds across great expanses of asphalt, rather than on the backs of horses. We work in artificial environments and breathe machine-recycled air.

Now is the time to remember we are an intricate part of nature. In our hurried lives, we have a tendency to lose touch with our natural rhythms and cycles. We have the power to make more intelligent choices for our planet, now and in the future. As individuals, we have the ability to tune into the ever-flowing, ever-renewing cycle of the Goddess. We are one with Her. From nature's examples, we can better understand the order and nature of our own existence and help heal the wounds of the Mother Goddess, the Earth. When we heal Her, we heal humankind. If we destroy Her, we destroy ourselves.

LEY LINES AND ANCIENT TRACKWAYS

A central element of the Celtic understanding of the Earth and her powers comes from the art of geomancy. Geomancy, akin to the Eastern art of feng shui, is based on ley lines. Like acupuncture meridians of the Goddess, ley, or holy, lines are normally invisible lines of power that crisscross the land, extending throughout the planet. Natural formations such as wells, rivers, and rock outcroppings are often situated on ley lines. The term *lay of the land* comes from the awareness of these lines of energy. Originally, they were used as thoroughfares, trackways, and sources of spiritual power.

Trackways or roads are ways through which we can connect to the ancient living traditions of the Celts. Paths, trackways, and roads represent the greatest magic we inherit from the earliest peoples. An ancient trackway, path, or road evokes in us the spirit and adventure of journeying and the experience of physically connecting to the Goddess, the Earth. When we walk the roads and paths our ancestors once tread, we remember our heritage and the inherent knowledge of the land.

Some roads and trackways were originally worn smooth by animals, then followed by humans. Others developed functionally, linking tribal areas to water sources, hunting grounds, and neighboring tribes. Ancient tracks that follow the ridges of the land became major trade routes. Sacred or religious sites are often found at the points of convergence of the trackways and roads we travel.

The Celts, like many ancient peoples, harnessed the power of ley lines by erecting places of worship, such as henges, temples, and monuments, at certain points along the lines. These sites reflected the Celts' evolving Earth-centered spirituality, which was based on the connection between people, the Earth, the sky, and the heavens.

STANDING STONES AND SACRED SITES
Evidence of the Celts' communion with nature and observance of annual cycles dots the British and Western

European countryside in the form of standing stones that measure the paths of the sun, moon, and celestial bodies in relation to the Earth. Even though there is no evidence that the Druids erected the standing stones, the Druids used them to influence and direct the energies of the Earth, moon, sun, and stars.

The Druids harnessed the ley lines, also called dragon veins, for particular spiritual purposes. The dragon represents the unleashed energies that activate standing stones and sacred sites. The dragon veins or ley lines connect the ancient sacred sites into one massive generator of energy. The Druids tapped into this generator, into the energy veins and the elemental powers that lay within. The wailing of dragons—an odd and eerie sound that can sometimes be heard at standing stones—may actually be the audible noise from these energetic veins.

The conductors of the ley, or dragon energy, are the henges, earthworks, standing stones, dolmens, menhirs, and barrows, the subtle and involved alignments of which are attuned to the nodal points of this global (and cosmic) energy. Each spiral carved on the standing stones conveys a wordless message, and those who have gone before have left light in every stone for us to follow.

Most stone circles and sacred sites are oriented to celestial bodies, most commonly to the sun, moon, and particular star constellations. Sacred places served as celestial clocks and astronomical observatories as well as spiritual power centers. The farther north a person travels on the Earth, the more the sun moves from north to south. Only on the equinoxes does the sun rise and set due east and west. If the ancient Celts had lived on the equator, the standing stones, in their present configuration, would have been of little or no use to them.

Every day people travel from all over the globe to visit the standing stones, megaliths, barrows, and sacred sites of Britain. Something about the energetic or spiritual quality of the sites keeps drawing people to them, much like a homing beacon. Some have suggested that the ley lines are actually the "Spirit Paths" of our ancestors, and if we could just remember how to tap into them, we would gain the wisdom and knowledge of the ancients.

Stonehenge

At Stonehenge, the most famous of more than nine hundred known standing-stone groups in Britain, the Druid priests and priestesses would align themselves with, communicate with, and work with the energy at the henges and other sacred sites. Originally called Caerdemanon, the standing stones at Stonehenge are considered to be a castle of the Gods, built sometime between 2800 B.C. and 2100 B.C. no one yet knows by whom. The ley, or dragon, power of this grouping of stones was raised by the Druids for weather control, enhancing crop growth, healing, and communication with the Sky-Gods.

The dragon evolved into a negative symbol in Western culture because its energies were no longer understood, could not be controlled, and created havoc and destruction. Serpents and dragons were associated with the Earth goddess; only later, as the Goddess was appropriated by Christianity, was the dragon identified as an aggressive male symbol.

In Celtic Europe, the word *dragon* meant chieftain, and the title *Pendragon* meant lord protector. The word was tied to the Druid cosmology of the Sky-Gods, which included the constellation Draco. Today, the image of the dragon is once again evocative of the wise protector and guardian of life's mysteries and treasures. Examples of this more positive image can be seen in the recent movies *Dragon Heart* and *Dragon World*.

Glastonbury Tor

Stonehenge lies on the most famous Earth ley line, St. Michael's Ley, which links the standing stones to Glastonbury Tor and Salisbury Cathedral. Glastonbury Tor is considered one of the sights of ancient Avalon. Sitting atop Glastonbury Tor, you can see a celestial zodiac carved into the English countryside.

Called the "Glassy Isle" and *"Ynis-Witrin,"* the Tor is a temple within the Earth that was reputedly once part of a Druid college where priestesses of the Great Mother were trained. The Tor serves as a portal to the Underworld of the Celts, and myth has it that the legendary God of the Wild Hunt, Gwynn Ap Nudd, lives in the Tor's hollow inner depths, within its tunnels and subterranean waterways. The Tor becomes active when its axis aligns with specific astronomical events, particularly the solstices, the equinoxes, and the days halfway in-between.

At the top of Glastonbury Tor stands a bell tower of an ancient church dedicated to Saint Michael. The practice of erecting Christian churches and monasteries on top of pagan Celtic sacred sites was common as Christianity swept through the British Isles. Christians did this not only to supplant paganism, but also to utilize the inherent spiritual power of the site.

New Grange

The most well-known of the megaliths of Western Europe

is New Grange in Ireland. The land, near a bend in the River Boyne (named for the Goddess), was sacred, as evidenced by New Grange and the many surrounding mounds and earthworks in the same vicinity. The Neolithic chamber at New Grange is more than forty-five feet high and two-hundred sixty-five feet in diameter. It has been reconstructed, but in ancient times, it was probably completely covered by white stones. The sun's rays, moonbeams, and shadows interact with the rock art throughout the site. Oriented toward the midwinter sunrise, it dates back to 3300 B.C., and its name comes from *an uamh greine*, or "cave of the sun."

New Grange is a spiritual center connected with the Tuatha De Dannan, one of the earliest peoples of Ireland, who settled in the hills of Tara. The chamber is considered to be a portal to the Otherworld, to Tir na N'Og, the Celtic Paradise. In fact, the chamber was used for spiritual journeys, for obtaining the wisdom of our ancestors and experiencing the rites of the rebirth of the sun (son).

New Grange was designed with the obvious purpose of framing the sun at particular times during the solar year. Decorated with symbols of the Goddess, such as lozenges, zigzags, cupmarks, chevrons, spirals, the owl, and the serpent, it was an inner sanctum constructed to invoke the Goddess, where the people could come to communicate with her. This site was the location of ritual activities for communicating with deity and connecting with the powerful regenerative powers of the Goddess.

THE CONCEPT OF ONENESS

The core of Celtic spirituality is the concept of oneness. This means that all things are one, whatsoever they may be. Contrasting with the usual religious and spiritual dogma of

Christianity, this open-ended concept forms the basis of all Celtic Druid magic.

Oneness is a state of mind. Your spiritual ability is directly proportional to your understanding of the concept of oneness. As you turn your mind to oneness more frequently, you will notice that the concept transforms from an intellectual idea into known "experience." The key is to be patient and just keep turning your mind to oneness, remembering you are an inseparable part of a living whole, the Earth, and ultimately, the cosmos.

One helpful exercise is to connect your being with the elements. Initiates in the Druid tradition are instructed to repeat a waking meditation over and over, while sitting, walking, driving, eating, and so forth, as a reminder that we are one with the elements.

Repeat aloud or silently: "My flesh and bones are the Earth; the Earth is my flesh and bones—we are one. My breath is the air; the air is my breath—we are one. My eyes are the light; the light is my eyes—we are one. My emotions are the water; the water is my emotions, we are one." The more you practice this meditation, the closer your rapport with the elements and the corresponding Goddess and God.

You can take this meditation a step further by applying it to flowers, plants, clouds, other people, animals, the moon, the sun, the stars, and, indeed, the entire cosmos. After all, we are the stars; the stars are us—we are one.

PATTERNING

Celtic mythology and ritual began as a way for the Celts to track and talk about the patterns affecting their everyday lives. Patterns are natural configurations that appear everywhere in nature and are found within the very cellular structure of our bodies. Universal and cosmic energetic patterns form the world as we perceive it. Accordingly, universal creation is mirrored or harmonized by physical, sexual, or generative forces, forms, and patterns in nature.

Pattern is also a term for discussing our intentions and expectations. The word *pattern* derives from the roots *pater*, meaning father and *patron*, meaning guardian and protector. Patterns are formulas, models, and designs used for making things. Positive, or "bright," patterns vitalize, heal, engender positivity, strengthen, and enrich. Negative, or "dark," patterns break and injure, creating havoc and disruption, and eventually weaken life patterns. The word *positive* derives from "to place," whereas the word *negative* derives from "to deny." You harvest that which you sow.

Use your previous patterns as a gauge to understand and improve your present and future. Study and learn from the past and from what has gone before. Pay close attention to all the steps and component parts of the pattern along the way. The Celtic people felt that freedom and the free will to create our own patterns in life was our sacred birthright and divine gift.

THE THREE EYES OF KERRIDWEN

The formula for creating any pattern in magic is called the Three Eyes of Kerridwen in Celtic Druid tradition. It consist of three basic steps—expectation, desire, and merging. The probable success of all magical work is dependent upon the clarity of your expectation, the strength and power of your desire, and the depth of your merge.

The difference between a "little magical work" and a "great magical work" is simply being able to control the Three Eyes without aid. Even so, you must remember one basic truth when you perform any work—an error in calculation will result in an error in situation. The error can be in any of the three factors, or Eyes. So be clear with your intention. Be sure you know what it is you actually want and for what you are patterning. Go deep within yourself to know whether you truly want it.

The secret to successful spiritual or magical work stems from these three factors:

1. *Expectation* designates the nature, character, and circumstances of the thing you want. Your expectation needs to be specific and succinct. Keep it simple. When applying the Three Eyes, set your expectation higher than you would normally.

2. *Desire* means how much you wish for, crave, and long for the thing you want. You gather motivation to create patterns through your cumulative desire, including emotions and sensations. The stronger your desire becomes, the stronger the pattern—all the better for the spiritual work at hand.

3. *Merging* is to become aware of the fact that you are One with All Things. Merging is the key to all spiritual work and evolution.

For example, you may choose to pattern for a romantic relationship. Your **expectation** would be to find the best possible partner in the near future. Your **desire** would be to have a positive, loving, and fulfilling relationship. This you would want with your body, mind, and soul. Desire this relationship so strongly that you can taste, touch, hear, see, and smell what it is like. When you **merge**, see yourself in the positive relationship. Be there and nowhere else for a few minutes. Then come back to "normal" reality and release your pattern into the universe with your intention and breath. Use your imagination and be creative. Other patterns to work on might be helping children in your community learn a skill, cultivating a healthy vegetable garden, writing a novel, or even obtaining a new computer system.

MERGING

The process of merging allows you to reach a level of synchronicity with all things, with the boundless, with the ground of being. The capabilities of the mind surpass our present conceptions. This uncharted potential of mind and moving mind can be tapped through merging.

The inherent energy of all things can be utilized by merging. As the key to every magical pattern, merging connects you with oneness and the divine light. When learning, you generally merge with the manifested universe, which is essentially comprised of the energies that already exist. As your skills advance and your perception and awareness expand, you merge with the unmanifested universe, which is a place of spontaneous creation and synchronicity that circumvents "natural law."

Contemplation of oneness gives you a deeper understanding of yourself. When you merge with oneness, suddenly you realize that you are boundless. From this perspective, personal achievement becomes an ongoing choice. The rapport you cultivate with the Goddess and God empowers you in every aspect of your life.

When you engage in the merging process, your mind generally moves through four veils, or levels. The primary level is one of vivid, eidetic images. Images shift, float, and seem meaningless. Mythical creatures from folklore appear to move with the merging mind. The land and structures appear richly detailed and brightly colored. Your senses are heightened. Light is more luminescent and scents more pungent. Music becomes more expansive and textures more detailed.

The next mind shift while merging is usually at a personal recollective stage, considered to be the edge between the conscious and unconscious aspects of your mind. You may feel you are falling into the void only to be reborn again, releasing the negativity of your past. Repressed emotions arise and you relive past events.

From the personal recollective stage of mind, a deeper merge shifts you to the next level, a higher symbolic state. You experience and act out symbolic initiations and explore personal myths using archetypal forms. Often, you feel a sense of continuity of things, as though the facets of your life are depicted by mythical heroines and heroes, Goddesses and Gods.

Druid tradition teaches three deep merges that lead to God(dess)hood. First, merge with the manifested universe and realize you are all things. Second, merge deeply with the unmanifested universe to a place where there is no self. Third, merge with both the manifested and unmanifested universes, discovering that they are one without connotation or distortion.

Sensations experienced when merging range from relaxation, peacefulness, and well-being to numbness, spinning, flying, or intense heaviness. Often during merging you find yourself energetically floating, becoming both everything and nothing at all while remaining completely aware. One technique for enhancing your merging experience is to use breath as a focus for deepening the merge. Breathe deeply, counting slowly to three as you inhale, holding your breath for three counts, and then exhaling completely to the count of three. Do this at least nine times to deepen the merge.

THE FOUR KEYS OF KNOWLEDGE

All successful patterns are constructed using the Four Keys, or "Wynds," of Knowledge, which are self-honesty, self-responsibility, wisdom, and love. These keys form a structure from which to work.

Self-honesty means being honest and truthful with yourself, even when you find yourself being untruthful with others. Self-responsibility means taking responsibility for yourself and creating positive and ecological patterns, i.e., steering your own vessel. Wisdom is the perfect love of the Goddess and the perfect peace of the God. Wisdom always comes before love in the Celtic Druid tradition, as love without wisdom never lasts. Love means the love of the Threefold adventure of birth, life, and death, of gaining rapport and oneness with divine light. Love is the love of positive patterns and the Bright Goddess.

The Wheel of the Year

Celtic rituals and celebrations closely follow the cycles of the sun, in keeping with the Celtic emphasis on the significance of nature's patterns.

THE EIGHT GREAT DAYS

The eight Great Days of power represent the eight-spoked Wheel of the Year. When the Wheel is turned sunwise (clockwise), it moves through the eight seasonal festivals of Yule, Bridget's Day, Hertha's Day, Beltane, Letha's Day, Lughnassad, Hellith's Day, and Samhain. Celtic spiritual tradition revolves around these Sabbats, which are celebrated on the eve of, rather than on, the actual Great Day. The ritual days remind us of the Golden One's (the sun's) progress through the seasons. The role of the Great Moons and the Great Days is to attune us to these reoccurring cycles of the land and heavens. The ancient Celts understood the wisdom within nature and based their timekeeping method on the positions of the sun, moon, and celestial bodies. They noticed that, depending upon the angle at which its luminous face is seen from Earth, the moon became an accurate means for measuring time, relative to the sun's position.

Beginning at the winter solstice, the Celts watched both the cycles of the sun and moon to determine when to plant, when to harvest, and when to celebrate the Gods. Knowing the proper times to plant, breed, and harvest enhanced their survival.

The lunar cycle, which is approximately twenty-nine and one-half days, is about eleven days short of the three hundred sixty-five and one-quarter day solar cycle.

Watching the north-south course of the sun at the stone circles at Stonehenge and Callanish, the Celts were able to observe the path of the sun as it moved through the Great Days.

The solar year divides naturally into eight equal portions, so the Druids designated the solstice and equinox points as four Great Days. Another four Great Days were calculated halfway between each of the first four. In this way, every forty-five days a Great Day was celebrated.

The sun and the moon were the largest celestial bodies in the sky. Most of the stone circles in Britain and Europe are sun and moon observatories as well as spiritual centers. They represent the trilogy of sun, moon, and Earth, a trilogy of paramount importance to the Celts.

The eight Great Days are symbols of the seasons and of the spirit, extending into the culture and politics of the Celtic people. Divisions of four represented the sacred renewal patterns of their world. Ireland, for example, was divided into four kingdoms, with the High King's sector situated in the center. Britain was similarly partitioned. The four Elemental Queens from each of these kingdoms (North, East, South, and West) mated with the High King, as it was his sacred duty and their sacred trust. Each one of the four queens was truly a Goddess of Sovereignty on Earth, and the power of the land passed through her to the High King.

THE PATH OF THE SUN
Yule—Winter Solstice

In Welsh Druidic Tradition, the first Great Day is Yule. The celebration and ritual starts just before midnight and ends shortly after. Yule is celebrated on the eve of the

Winter Solstice, honoring the return of the sun and the lengthening days. At this time Tarvos, the Golden One, rises from the dust. The Goddess hears humankind's plea and returns the God to the land, bringing hope for the greening.

The symbolic rebirth of Tarvos is represented by a lighted live evergreen tree. In past times, the live potted tree was decorated with candles. Three women, representing the Maiden, Mother, and Crone, lit the candles with concentrated care. Nowadays, we use electric lights, and it is customary for a woman, representing the Goddess, to plug them in during the Yule ritual. The next morning, the live tree is planted.

Burning the Yule log is also traditional. The Celts believed that a piece of the Yule log, if kept safe, would protect the house, secure a bountiful harvest, and aid the livestock in birthing. Spreading holly branches on the fireplace mantel and hanging mistletoe suggest similar fertility themes.

On Yule, take a piece of paper, and on it write the thing you would most like to eliminate in your life. Take the paper, rip it up, and burn it in the Yule fire, with the intention of ridding yourself of the burden. Yule gifts are exchanged as symbols of love and renewal. At the end of the ritual, it is traditional to dance a circle dance, while calling out the names of favorite Goddesses and Gods, chanting their names over and over.

Bridget's Fire (Imbolc)—February 2

On this Great Day, we honor the sun Goddess Bridget, who is the patroness of hearth and home, of poets and artisans, and of smiths and craftsmen. Groundhog Day is an offshoot of Bridget's Day. Bridget's name means "Bright One" and she is the sacred bride. In ancient times, Bridget's temple was the sanctuary of the sacred fire, representing the elemental fire of the sun. This fire was only allowed to burn out once each year on the eve of Bridget's Fire. The next morning, the High Priestess lit a new fire out of nine types of wood. This newly ignited fire was the "need-fire."

Across the countryside, households let their fires die out on Bridget's eve. The next day, women went to Bridget's temple to gather the sacred fire. They would light a branch from the fire, take it home and start their hearth fires. As they lit their fires, they chanted, "Bridget, Bridget, Bridget, brightest flame. Bridget, Bridget, Bridget, sacred name!"

Fruit trees are planted at Bridget's Fire as a symbol of the fruitful and fertile Goddess. On the Isle of Man, the head of the household asks a family member to wait outside the front door and hands the person a potted fruit tree to hold. The family members inside the house call out, "Bridget, Bridget, Bridget, come to my house, come to my house tonight. Open the door for Bridget, and let Bridget come in." The person outside knocks loudly three times. The door is opened and the fruit tree is brought inside, and pampered for the evening. The next morning, on Bridget's Day, the tree is planted.

Hertha's Day (Ostara)—Spring Equinox

Tarvos, the Golden One, is born on Hertha's Day, also called Lady's Day. The word Earth is derived from Hertha's name, as she acts as Mother to Tarvos and symbolizes the land itself. Tarvos (the sun) is born at Coventina's Well, which is representative of the womb of the Earth Mother.

Seeds are customarily planted on Hertha's Day, as a tribute to the Goddess and the spring greening. The fertile Earth

Goddess and her son, a young God, are honored, as all nature breaks forth in joy. The birds sing their sweetest songs, and the animals gather around eagerly awaiting the birth of the Golden One, the sun. As the days grow longer, the Goddess and God awaken and herald the beginning of spring.

Beltane—May Day

Beltane is also called the "Adventure of the Sun." This Great Day begins at moonrise on May Day eve, and marks the bright half of the year, symbolized by the Bright Goddess. In Celtic tradition, the Beltane bonfire is lit with the spark from friction or flint. Contact with the fire, by jumping over or through it, symbolizes purification by the life-giving sun. People dance the Celtic Holy Round clockwise around the sacred bonfire, and cattle are driven through the fire to increase the fertility of the herds and prevent disease. Rowan or oak branches and twigs are carried three times, sunwise, around the Beltane bonfire for protection and good fortune.

The celebration of Beltane is one of fertility, and thus May is considered the month of sexual license. Couples would often make love in the fields on Beltane as a way to ensure the harvest. A springtime "greening" ritual, dancing around the Maypole, honors the female and male principles of regeneration and creation. The May Queen and King literally and figuratively represent the Goddess and God.

Letha's Day (Midsummer)—Summer Solstice

On Midsummer's morning on the Isle of Lewis in the Outer Hebrides when the sun rises, legend tells of the "Shining One" who walks through the ancient stone avenue dressed in a robe of bird feathers. The cuckoo, bird of Tir na N'Og, heralds the shining sun's arrival on the longest day of the year.

The Summer Solstice is named Letha's Day, "Letha" meaning death—in this instance, the slow death of the sun. Midsummer begins the "dark" half of the year. From Letha's Day to Yule, the days grow shorter and the nights longer. Lugh, the Underworld God identified with the moon, rules this six-month period.

Lughnassad—First Week of August

Lughnassad is a harvest ritual, commemorating the wedding feast of the master God, Lugh, and Rosemerta, the Rose Mother. Nassad means "to give in marriage." Lugh's wedding celebration honors the ascendancy of the moon. Held just after sunset on the eve of Lughnassad, the ritual marks the convergence of the forces of light and dark. Two portals occur, one just prior to sunset and one immediately after the sun goes down.

At Teltown on the River Boyne, an ancient Celtic festival commemorated Lugh's foster mother, Taillte. Lughnassad is a memorial to her death and her symbolic rebirth. At "the Hollow of the Fair," couples are married, embodying the union of the sun and Earth. When the Goddess weds the sun, as she does at Beltane, she marries life. When she weds Lugh, the Underworld God, she marries death. The Goddess gleans all of the knowledge of the Underworld through her union with death.

The destruction of the Corn Mother symbolizes the death of the Goddess. This ritual is held on Lughnassad, Hellith's Day, and/or Samhain. Considered sacred and holy, the last corn sheaf is drenched in water and kept as an emblem of the Goddess and continued abundant harvest.

Hellith's Day (Mabon)—Autumnal Equinox

Starting after sunset on the eve of the Autumnal Equinox, Hellith's Day is the last day of bringing the harvest home. Hellith's Day celebrations have been continuously observed throughout the ages and still thrive in areas of rural Britain. Everyone participates in the festivities, such as the destruction of the Corn Mother, feasting, stories, and music. Other names for this Great Day were the "Inning" or "Ingathering" or in Scotland, "the Kern."

The Autumnal Equinox is associated with death, when light and dark, day and night are equal. The God Hellith symbolizes the dying sun, the last harvests of the season, and a time of gathering seeds before the cold winter. *Hell* comes from the root of Hellith's name. The ancient Celts did not perceive "Hel" or "Hell" to be a place of punishment, but an Otherworld inhabited by those who died of disease or old age.

Samhain—Halloween

Celebrated after sunset, Samhain literally means "the end of summer" and is associated with the beginning of winter and the sleeping Earth Goddess. It is a time of death, the dark part of the year, and is ruled by the Dark Goddess and her consort. On this Great Day, legend says that the Great Sea Mother, the Morrigan, made love with the Good God, the Dagda, where the rivers come together.

The veil between dimensions of time and space draws to its thinnest point at Samhain. The portal is open to the Otherworlds, and the spirits of the departed can more readily communicate with the living on Samhain eve. Contact with deities is also easier. Stories are told of people who pass through the portals on Samhain and return to tell their extraordinary tales or who never return. In Ireland, the Faery hills are thrown open and the Faery troop forth to mingle with humankind.

Traditionally, messages from the departed or from deities are conveyed to those who gather together on Samhain. By drawing lots, the Druids would choose a person to serve as the "Oracle of Death." This person would then sit in a quiet, dark location and answer questions about the future. An example of the knowledge the Oracle imparted would be messages from your ancestors.

The "Dumb Supper," a feast for the spirits, is also a Samhain eve custom. Plates loaded with food and drink are put outside the door in the dark of night, with lighted red and white candles standing on the ground around the plates. Any food or drink that remains the next morning is given to the Earth, to the Goddess.

THE PATH OF THE MOON
Lunar and stellar cycles are in tune with the eight Great Days of the solar cycle. The purpose of ritual and celebration on the High (full) Moons is to attune our sensitivities to the phases, or as the Celts called it, the "Path of the Moon" and the Goddess of the Silver Wheel of the Stars. The moon is the embodiment of the Goddess, as exemplified in the correlation between the twenty-eight-day cycle of the moon and the female menstrual cycle.

The phases of the moon, caused by the changing angle of its lighted surface as seen from the Earth, form one of humankind's best time-keeping methods. From observing the lunar cycles, the Druids devised a calendar of twelve half-months of fifteen nights each, and twelve half-months of fourteen nights each. Three and one-quarter nights

72

remained every year. These odd nights were lucky or unlucky, depending upon their placement in the calendar.

Starting with the first full, or high, moon after Yule, the Path of the Moon consists of thirteen moons; either the full or new moon cycles thirteen times within a given year. The names of the thirteen moons of Celtic Druid tradition are the Wolf, Storm, Chaste, Seed, Hare, Dyad, Mead, Wort, Barley, Wine, Blood, Snow, and Oak.

All water and fluids on the Earthly plane are influenced by the moon, including the fluids within our bodies. Welsh tradition says that people are born when the ocean tide comes in and die when the tide goes out.

Lunar positioning and phase influences the deep water of feeling and emotion, as well as instinct, sensation, fertility, maternity, imagination, and receptivity. Each High Moon rises in a particular zodiac sign, strongest in the zodiac sign of Cancer. Every moon has its own unique aspects, reflecting different seasonal combinations of energies that can be tapped into and used in ritual and celebration.

The moon and Earth are mirrors of the sun, which is actually a star. On the full moon, the moon and sun are positioned exactly opposite each other. Eclipses of the moon occur only on the full moon when the earth travels between the sun and the moon. A Blue Moon occurs when two High Moons rise within the same month.

The Eight-Fold Moon Phase
The eight-fold monthly moon phase cycle mirrors the Celtic eight Great Days as follows:

MOON PHASE	CORRESPONDING GREAT DAY
New Moon	Yule (Winter Solstice)
Crescent Moon	Bridget's Day (February 2)
First Quarter Moon	Hertha's Day (Spring Equinox)
Gibbous Moon	Beltane (May Day)
Full Moon	Letha's Day (Summer Solstice)
Disseminating Moon	Lughnassad (First Week of August)
Last Quarter Moon	Hellith's Day (Fall Equinox)
Balsamic/Dark Moon	Samhain (Halloween)

The Celts understood the natural cycles of the moon. They used these cycles and qualities in their lives and knew the waxing moon was the time for building energy while the waning moon was the time for releasing energy. Traditionally, from the new moon to the first quarter moon is a time to initiate and build patterns, to clarify your intent and expectation. From the first quarter to the full moon becomes the time to cultivate the patterns you have created and to gather the energy needed for their successful completion. The full moon is called the High Moon because the lunar energies are at their strongest and highest. The last quarter of the moon corresponds to harvest time, when you reap the rewards of your efforts. The last quarter through the dark moon and into the new moon is traditionally a time to explore the mysteries of life, rebirth, dreams, and the stars.

Symbology of the Thirteen Moons
Each full moon has certain qualities or aspects that serve as seasonal guidelines for ritual and celebration. This list begins with the first High Moon after Yule. Oak Moon is

not used in years that have only twelve full-moons.

Wolf Moon: unity, purity, and dormancy

The first full moon after Yule is called the Wolf Moon; it is a time of self-responsibility and self-honesty. Celtic folklore says that if you gaze into the face of the first full moon of the year, you may see your future lover. The Celts believed that the weather for the first twelve days after the Wolf Moon was indicative of the weather for the next year, one day representing each month.

The wolf and raven work together in the wild, communicating and sharing food as a way to survive. Wolves howl at the full moon, reaffirming their wildness. They also hunt and play in the moonlight. Several Celtic Goddesses and Gods, such as Medb and Merlin, had the wolf as their emblem. Legend has it many of them shapeshifted into the wolf on the full moon.

Storm Moon: duality and polarity (as above, so below)

The Storm Moon is a time of polarity and duality, a time of of stirring up energy (as in stirring the cauldron). Storms bring change, both positive and negative. The Druids were renowned for raising the winds and fogs, leveling hills, and drying up rivers and lakes. Celtic people used singing, whistling, chanting, and drumming to control the weather and the forces of storms. The Goddess Bridget is credited for introducing the art of whistling to humankind, and the seafaring Celtic people practiced whistling-up-the-wind in order to sail over the waterways and seas.

A large body of folklore is related to storms and the weather (as above, so below). For example: If there is a halo around the moon, it will rain; when stars appear in the halo's ring, rain will continue for several days. When there are less than five stars within the ring, the weather will be warmer; when more than five stars, the temperature will be cold.

The Chaste Moon: trinity of the Maiden, Mother, and Crone

Virtuous words and actions, together with clear and pure intent, symbolize the Chaste Moon. Purity in this sense indicates a lunar strength, free from imperfection and things that hinder, impair, and weaken it—an energetic strength.

The Chaste Moon is the third full moon of the cycle and thus symbolizes the Celtic trinity of Maiden, Mother, and Crone. The Triple Goddess and Threefold One carries many meanings: birth, life, and death; new moon, waxing moon, and waning moon; creation, destruction, and regeneration; past, present, and future; and positive, neutral, and negative. The trinity reminds us of the concept of oneness—that all fragments combine to create the whole. In fact, they cannot be truly separated, as the parts are like cells of the body of the Goddess, the Great Mother, Earth.

The Seed Moon: the solidity of the four elements of manifestation

The four elements of manifestation, earth (north), air (east), fire (south), and water (west), are represented by the fourth moon, the Seed Moon. All patterns consist of these elements, with you, the practitioner, acting as the fifth element, or conduit of spirit. When working with elemental energies, remind yourself that you are an embodiment of the elements.

The Seed Moon is a time to plant seeds in your personal life as well as in the garden. Seeds are ovules from which all life stems. Within a seed are the combined energies of oneness: birth, life, death, and rebirth. The Celtic people understood that the growth of the seed was dependent upon the initial seed quality and upon environmental factors such as the timing of the planting, sunlight, water, and care. They knew planting cycles were based on moonlight. During the full moon, they planted the crops that grew above the ground, and during the dark of the moon, they planted root crops.

The Hare Moon: control of the self, the physical manifestation

The hare is an important totem animal, familiar in Celtic folklore and mythology, which serves as the badge for first-degree initiates in Welsh Druid Tradition. Mary Queen of Scots also used the hare as her personal emblem. The Iceni Warrior Queen, Boudicca kept a hare within her cloak and unleashed the animal when she went to battle the invading Romans. Shapeshifters change into hares, cats, and birds more than any other animals.

The Hare moon is a time of learning control over our physical manifestations. *Hara*, which means "the seat of power," is the root of the word *hare*.

The Dyad Moon: time, multi-dimensions, boons

The sixth full moon is halfway along the Path of the Moon, at the point where the energies of light and darkness meet. The Dyad Moon is called the "Boon Moon" in Druid Tradition. The Goddess grants you a gift, or boon, depending upon your works during the previous year. Symbolic of time, the Dyad Moon serves as a gateway through time and space, a portal to other dimensions, such

77

as the home of the Celtic Goddesses and Gods, the Land of Promise, Tir na N'Og.

The word *dyad* stems from the Greek word *dyas*, meaning the number two. The Dyad Moon embodies the strengthening force of two—mortal human joined with deity. Similarly, a dyad is defined as an element, atom, or radical that has a combining power of two—that which is doubled or paired.

The Mead Moon: lunar fertility, dreams, etheric link

The Mead Moon is a time of vivid and lucid dreams, lunar fertility, and etheric harmony. This is the ideal time to keep a dream journal or tape-record your dreams for later reference and use. Great joy and love are afoot at this High Moon.

Mead is the name of the heavenly drink of the old Teutonic Gods. The Celts were connoisseurs of the elixir and rivers and lakes of mead flow throughout Scottish and English ballads. Mead, probably the first fermented beverage ever made by humankind, is considered to have medicinal and healing qualities.

The Wort Moon: the yearly cycle

The yearly cycle and the eight Great Days are represented on the eighth full moon. The Wort Moon is a time of predicting the seasonal cycles of the upcoming year by examining the signs of seeding, cultivation, growth, and early harvests, and by observing the movements of the stars.

The wort is a type of plant or herb, such as pennywort and navelwort. In the brewing of beer, the wort is an infusion of malted barley combined with hops and special grains. The wort is combined with the yeast, springs to life, and eventually transforms into beer. The Celts made beer only in the summer because of the warm temperatures required for successful brewing.

The Barley Moon: wisdom and knowledge

The Barley Moon is a night of magic, healing, and wisdom. Barley, with its triple spikelets, is the oldest of foods. The first cereal ever cultivated, barley was a food staple as hunting cultures evolved into agrarian societies. In Celtic societies, women directed the planting of the barley seeds, cultivated, harvested, and dried the grain. The grain was stored, used for making bread, used medicinally for healing, and malted for brewing beer.

Common in Celtic rituals, barley was honored at births, initiations, weddings, and funerals. Similar to the Corn Mother, the Barley Mother symbolizes the ever-renewing cycle of life. When the Goddess weds death, as the Barley Mother does, she renews herself. That which is born never dies, but is reborn.

Wine Moon: prophecy

The Wine Moon is a time of prophecy. The gift of prophecy comes from the ability to merge with spirit, as well as from observing and reading patterns in life. Often prophecy is made under divine influence or intervention, and intoxication was one way the Celts let go and connected with the Goddess and God.

Wine, the oldest of medicines, also serves as a menstruum in medicinal preparations. The human body absorbs herbs much more quickly if the ingredients are first dissolved in wine.

The Blood Moon: maternity and fecundity
The Blood Moon is the ancestral moon, honoring the maternal qualities of the Goddess. The Celts believed that the spirit of a person resides in her/his blood. Blood is life itself. Our blood actually mirrors the salinity of Earth's oceans. The Holy Grail is a life-giving vessel, as it holds the divine blood, just as the Goddess is a living vessel who holds the blood of the Earth.

Specific groups such as the Irish Red Branch and King Arthur and the Knights of the Round Table were joined through covenants of blood. Through ritual, they become loyal to one another, of one blood and family, as if they were joined by ancestry.

The Snow Moon: divine or royal purpose
The Snow Moon represents divine or royal purpose and the sovereignty of the land. It becomes a time for developing your divine or royal inner awareness. The sovereigns of the ancient Celts were spiritual leaders as well as rulers of the people. They embodied the power of the Goddess and God on the Earthly plane through divine birthright, while connecting to the very sacredness of the land itself. When the land and the people thrived, the sovereigns thrived and vice versa.

The last High Moon in twelve-full-moon years, the Snow Moon symbolizes the potential of things, much like the frozen water necessary for life that waits for the thaw.

The Oak Moon: the lunar cycle, rebirth, and transmigration
As the thirteenth Moon, the Oak Moon embodies the lunar cycle, the creative process of birth and expansion as well as

transmigration, regeneration, and rebirth. The word *Druid* translates as "Oak Seer," as all knowledge and wisdom resides within the roots and belly of the oak. Symbolizing strength, endurance, and fertility, the last leaf of the oak never falls, and its acorns served as a food staple for the Celts. Vast evergreen and oak forests once covered Europe and the British Isles. Most worshipped of all trees, the oak was the first tree created, from which sprang humankind. Need-fires and the traditional Yule Log are still kindled from the sacred oak.

Mistletoe gathered from the oak was considered the most powerful all-heal by the Druids. They gathered it on the Summer and Winter Solstices by knocking the plant out of the tree with a rock or stick and catching it in a white cloth before it touched the ground. Mistletoe, which bestows fertility and represents the "life of the oak," was used traditionally for protection, healing, heightened sensitivity, and spiritual knowledge.

Celtic Ritual and Ceremony

Ritual and symbol speak to the unconscious; they are ways to tap into the creative power of the Goddess. Ritual consists of setting up the altar, drawing the sacred circle, working with the elemental powers of nature, gaining rapport with the Goddess and God, and practicing healing works.

Repeated through generations and time, ritual becomes a powerful change element for self-discovery and development, where energies mate and combine. Celtic Earth-centered ritual attunes you to the flow of nature while increasing your inner awareness. Each time you engage in ritual you merge with the Goddess and God, which connects you with oneness and the natural cycles of the Earth, moon, sun, and stars.

Rituals offer time to gather people together to celebrate the Goddess and direct divine light and consciousness. They help keep us aware of and attuned with the seasons and nature's cycles. The purpose of Celtic ritual is to participate in and perpetuate the regulation of the natural cycles of birth, life, death, and rebirth, to help the Great Mother grow and thrive.

RITUAL BASICS
Setting up the Altar

The altar is a fundamental part of Celtic ritual. Each element is represented on the altar by sacred tools, which are traditionally consecrated by the Goddess and God during the initiation rituals on the High Moons or Great Days. Through intention and constant use, altar tools take on a "magical" quality.

To set up an altar, first carefully select your altar tools, which include: Goddess and God symbols, wand, chalice or cup, bowl, *athame* (with dulled edges), incense holder, robe with ten-foot cord (optional), altar cloth, wine cup, three candle holders and three candles (white, green, and red).

Setting your altar is a personal experience, so experiment and use the placement that works the best. An altar can be a simple piece of ground or a rock or an elaborate table of statues and symbols. Cover the surface with a green or red altar cloth with symbols of the Goddess, such as spirals, stars, moons, and suns. Position your tools so you can move them easily, and on a sturdy surface in the North point.

Altar tools symbolize the four elements, and you, the practitioner, represent the fifth element of spirit. The traditional Druid placement of altar tools on the altar follows. Looking at your altar and facing the North point, first place the Goddess symbols on the left and the God symbol on the right, toward the center back portion of the surface. Goddess and God symbols can be statues, rocks, plants, or anything you choose. Place a green candle in a candle holder on the left-hand side of the altar, next to the Goddess symbol, and put a red candle in a candle holder on the right-hand side, next to the God symbol.

The Goddess, or left, side of the altar holds the feminine nurturing elements of water and earth, symbolized by the bowl of salt and chalice of water. The wand, preferably one you have made yourself, rests on the Goddess side of the altar as well. The wine (or juice) cup, a symbol of divine love, sits at the center of the altar.

The God, or right side of the altar, holds the power elements. These are the white candle of the Goddess (symbol of fire) and an incense burner (symbol of the air). The *athame* (ceremonial knife) is also placed on the male, or hot, side of the altar.

Drawing the Sacred Circle

In Celtic custom, a man representing the God performs the preliminary rituals of "Drawing the Sacred Circle" and "Calling in the Four Watchtowers." A woman, representing the Great Goddess, hands him the elements of energy. These elements symbolize the tools of infinite potential. Woman holds the power and man wields the light. Woman and man represent polarities of energy, aspects of Oneness. If you are working alone, you don the roles of both Goddess and God.

Draw the sacred circle as a means of protection from negative influences every time you do ritual. These are the five steps:

1. Visualize or sense a clear cobalt-blue light washing out the room as you say aloud, "May all evil and foulness be gone from this place. I ask this in the Lady's name. Be gone, now and forever more." Do this three times, turning in a sunwise circle and sweeping the area with your mind.

2. With your *athame*, draw a clockwise circle around your ritual area, visualizing a blue-white flame flaring out of the blade.

3. Purify the four corners with salt, starting at the North Point, and chanting, "Ayea, Ayea Kerridwen! Ayea, Ayea Kernunnos! Ayea, Ayea, Ayea!" After purifying the North point, continue on to the East, South, and West points, in that order.

4. After moving around the four corners of the circle, face the altar and say in a firm voice, "Blessed Be! Blessed Be the Gods! Blessed Be all who are gathered here."

5. Merge with the Goddess, and knock nine times on the altar with the handle of your *athame*, your wand or your knuckles, in three series of three knocks.

Your Sacred Circle is now set in place until you close it.

Calling in the Watchtowers

After you set the Sacred Circle in place, call in the Watchtowers, or Four Wards, to stand guard at each of the four corners during ritual. The procedure is as follows:

1. After the Sacred Circle is drawn, bring the altar tools into the center of the circle.
2. Take the bowl of salt or earth and stand at the North point. Sprinkle a bit of salt or earth on the ground.
3. Set the bowl down, and holding your *athame* in your right hand and lifting both of your arms, say aloud, "Oh, great and mighty one, ruler of the North March, come, I pray you. Protect the gate of the North Ward. Come, I summon you!" Set down your *athame* (either back on the altar or on a safe spot on the ground).
4. Take the lighted incense burner in your hands and stand at the East point. Move the burner back and forth in front of you three times. Set the burner down and with your *athame* in your right hand, hold up your arms and say, "Oh, great and mighty one, ruler of the East March, come, I pray you. Protect the gate of the East Ward. Come, I summon you!" Set down your *athame*.
5. Take the candle holder with lighted white candle and stand at the South point. Wave the candle three times across the South point. Set the candle down carefully, and with your *athame* in your right hand, hold your arms upward and say, "Oh great and mighty one, ruler of the South March, come, I pray you. Protect the gate of the South Ward. Come, I summon you!" Set down your *athame*.

6. Take the chalice of water and stand at the West point. Sprinkle nine drops (in three series of three) on the ground and set the chalice down. Hold your *athame* in your right hand and holding your arms upward, say, "Oh great and mighty one, ruler of the West March, come, I pray you. Protect the gate of the West Ward. Come, I summon you!" Set down your *athame*. The four Wards are now standing guard.

7. Move to the circle center and begin to chant the names of your favorite Goddesses and Gods. For example, "Kerridwen, Kerridwen, Kerridwen! Kernunnos, Kernunnos, Kernunnos! Ayea, Ayea, Ayea!" Build the power up and then direct the energy toward the work or healing of your choice. Swaying or dancing enhances the final power build-up.

Cutting the Little Gate

After the Four Wards are called into the circle, the man cuts a "Little Gate," an energetic gate, just below the East point. The woman removes the four elements (the tools) from the circle. If you are working with a group, the others now enter the circle through this gate. The man then closes the gate with his *athame*, handing it back to the woman, who places the *athame* back upon the altar.

Toasting the Gods and Feasting

After the rituals on the Great Days and High Moons, it is the Celtic custom to toast the Goddesses and Gods. Participants fill their glasses with drink and select favorite Goddesses and Gods to toast. For instance, you might raise your glass and say, "To Danu, Ayea, Great Mother."

Feasting is also traditional after the Great Day rituals. A special meal is prepared and eaten after the ritual by all those who partake. Feasting was one of the gifts the Dagda, the Good God, gave to humankind. The feast is a sacred meal in honor of the Goddess and God, and topics related to spirituality and magic are discussed in round-table style by all those present.

Closing the Circle

At the end of the ritual, thank the Goddess and God for their rapport, kindness, and assistance. Use your *athame* to pull up the Sacred Circle. Holding your *athame* out in front of you, pointed outward, visualize the blue-white light of the circle being sucked into the blade. Move in a 360-degree counterclockwise circle when doing this procedure. Knock three times on the altar in honor of the Triple Goddess and to release the circle. Leave the area immediately. The ritual is complete.

FULL MOON HEALING RITUAL

Traditionally, High Moon healing rituals begin after dark. Healing rituals can be done with a group of people or alone. The customary greeting when working with a healing group is "Merry Met and Merry Part; Perfect Love and Perfect Peace."

Begin the ritual by setting up your altar and healing space. Decide who or what is to be healed and focus your attention there. Place your tools in their appropriate positions, light the incense and candles, fill the chalices with water and wine (juice), and place salt or earth in your altar bowl. You may choose to add some special background music, scented oils, certain foods, and special lighting for your ritual.

Be clear as to your intention and expectation in the healing ritual. Build your desire for a successful healing, and make an effort to merge as deeply as you can with the Goddess and God of your choice. Become one with deity.

Start to chant the names of the Goddesses and Gods you have selected to help you. The Goddess and God names are chanted three times or nine times. Use alternating female and male deities in your chanting pattern. For example, if you chose Bridget, Lugh, and Nimue to be your healing sponsors, chant, "Bridget, Bridget, Bridget! Lugh, Lugh, Lugh! Nimue, Nimue, Nimue! Ayea, Ayea, Ayea!"

Merge as deeply as you can with deity and bring the energy within and outside of your body to a peak. As you chant, allow the healing energy to come through you into its destination. When you are finished directing the healing energy, say, "Blessed Be. Blessed Be the Gods." Swaying, low vocal tones, textures, the environment, and the people around you all influence the healing ritual. The manner in which you draw your circle and perform the preliminaries all figure into the success of the healing ritual.

Divination Tools
and Practices

SYMBOL-CONCEPT LANGUAGES

During ritual, divination tools were used by the Celts to predict future patterns and events. Each of these tools acts as a triggering device. With intention and deep merging, the strength and wisdom of the Goddess and God are communicated through the symbols of the tools. This is termed symbol-concept language, where knowledge is communicated through the symbols themselves rather than through words.

Symbol-concept languages used by the Celts to foretell the future include divining wands, feather augury, oghams, and tarot, as well as astrology, numerology, palmistry, and runes. Being able to forecast the future enhanced survival and offered a way to connect with the Goddess and God. When you divine the future, you tap into the source, to deity and divinity. Divination tools and symbol-concept languages can be used to expand your awareness, inner wisdom, inner guidance, insight, and clarity. However, remember not to become dependent upon divination tools or base your life solely on the prophesies that arise. Be sure to look at the larger picture.

DRYAMANCY WANDS

The Druid divination art called "Dryamancy" is the use of Divining Wands as a means to predict the future. The framework behind Dryamancy is that within every tree lives a spirit, or Dryad. The Druids purported that the Tree Dryads were created by the first rays of the sun, long before human beings were on the Earth. With the help of the Dryads, humans were then formed. Without the trees and their Dryads, the Druids knew, the Earth would not survive.

When you cut your Dryamancy Wands, choose a tree with a strong spirit that resonates with yours or one that has the qualities you require for divining. It is the Celtic custom to ask the tree spirit's permission before taking its wood, returning all shavings and unused pieces in a sunwise pattern around the base of the tree when you are finished making your wands.

Fashion seven Divining Wands from the wood you have taken: three rods nine inches long, three thirteen inches long, and one special wand of any length (your choice) that is clearly marked. Often one's altar wand is used as the special wand. Decorate and energetically charge your Divining Wands to your specifications. To charge the wands with energy, visualize a bright white light coming from the Goddess and God into your Divining Wands. Put your wands together in a cloth bag or box when you are not using them and recharge them frequently, especially just before use.

To use your Divining Wands, lay the special wand horizontally on the floor or ground in front of you. Hold the other six wands in your right hand about two feet above the special wand on the ground. Close your eyes, and mix the six wands around while thinking of your question or wish. Next merge with oneness, with the Goddess and God, and allow your wish or question to completely flood your mind and being. With your left hand, take hold of the tip of one of the wands you are holding and allow the remainder of them to fall to the ground. Read the wands as follows:

1. If more long wands fall to the ground, the answer to your question is yes, and your wish will come true.
2. If more short wands fall to the ground, the answer to your question is no.
3. The answer is even more definitive if one or more of the wands falls to the ground and touches the special wand.
4. If any of the wands is not touching the ground (perched on top of the others), recast the wands.
5. If the wands all point to the special wand, you will have a hand in the outcome of the question or wish.
6. If none of the wands point to the special wand, then the matter will be settled without your intervention.

Customary Divining Woods

Alder . . . . The "battle witch" of trees. Represents truth as purification by fire.

Ash . . . . The "guardian tree," dispenser of justice, associated with runes.

Elder . . . . The "thirteenth tree," representing Kerridwen.

Hazel . . . . The tree of Wisdom. Cuts away impurities to see self honestly.

Ivy . . . . Grows in a sacred spiral, symbolizes strength.

Laurel . . . . . . The Oracle tree of Delphi. Represents victory and honor.

Mistletoe . . . . The all-heal, best in questions of healing and trustworthiness.

Oak . . . . The "Forest King" of endurance and the primary wood of Bridget's sacred fire. Associated with fertility, ancestry, and love.

Pine . . . . Represents cycle of life and rebirth. Tree of the Manifest, the Sun.

Rowan . . . . . . The "Wood of the Sorcerer," its pliability is thought to aid in enchantment.

Silver Fir . . . . Lunar associations, feminine rebirth.

Willow . . . . . . The "Tarvos Tree," flexible and good in enchantment, draws from water.

Yarrow . . . . . . Also called "Milfoil," the most popular wood used for Divining Wands; all-heal, called the medicine of life.

THE OGHAMS

Sacred to the Druids, the Ogham script used by the Celts until A.D. 700 served as an alphabet, a secret form of communication, a divination tool, and also as the Celtic Tree Calendar. It was considered a living alphabet. One of the Tuatha De Dannan, Ogma, a God of poetry, speech, and eloquence, is credited with inventing the ancient Ogham alphabet. Divided into three subgroups of Chieftains, Peasants, and Shrubs, the Ogham is a system of notches (vowels) and lines (consonants) based on the qualities of nature, particularly the hierarchy of trees. The sacred alphabet reflected the mystical connection with trees and nature, as each of the Ogham letters represented a different type of tree or shrub, with the exception of the Grove and the Sea Oghams.

The Ogham notches and lines were cut into divining sticks, candles, stones, trees, monuments, and also spelled out silently with parts of the body. You can still see Ogham markings on the sacred sites in Britain, cut into rough tombs and monuments. Many who study and practice Celtic spirituality today carry on the tradition by learning to use the ancient Oghams.

Hand, Nose, and Shin Ogham

The Hand Ogham, Nose Ogham, and Shin Ogham are all forms of covert sign language that were used by the Celts. These forms of Ogham were particularly useful during meetings and negotiations because those who knew the Ogham could communicate with each other silently and secretly, while simultaneously conversing normally with foreign powers, merchants, or enemies. Socially and politically, this gave the Celts an advantage.

The Hand Ogham uses a particular finger joint to designate each letter by pointing to or displaying each joint to spell words. Letters can also be made with the fingers themselves. The Hand Ogham was used as a divination tool for forecasting by concentrating on the location of sensations on the hand and fingers while asking questions.

The Nose Ogham uses the nose as a baseline and the five fingers (four plus thumb) to form the letters on the nose in the four groups.

The Shin Ogham uses the shin bone to represent the baseline. The individual letters are formed in the same way as in the Nose Ogham.

Ogham Sticks

The ancient Celts had a strong kinship with trees. Expressions like "knocking on wood" and "touching wood three times" are by-products of the fellowship between people and tree spirits. In fact, knocking on wood was considered the best way to awaken the spirit within the tree. Ogham sticks are a divination tool that makes use of this fellowship. The modern game of pick up sticks is a direct descendent of the Ogham sticks, only the sacred and magical meanings of the sticks are no longer part of the game.

As mentioned previously, it is customary to ask the tree spirit, or Dryad, permission to use its wood before cutting your sticks from the tree. If you don't have access to living trees, you can use popsicle sticks or tongue depressors. To make Ogham sticks, first gather and shape twenty-one same-sized sticks. The twenty-first stick is left unnotched and acts as a "wild card." Engrave or paint each of the other twenty sticks with the signs of the Ogham alphabet, one sign per stick. Put your Ogham sticks in a box or bag, and then draw three, seven or nine sticks without looking. In your mind, go over your question or the issue at hand, and then toss the Ogham sticks on the ground. The sticks farthest from you indicate the future outcome of the question. The sticks landing closest to you are representative of present influences. Any sticks that touch other sticks, or lay on top of other sticks, have a direct connection to each other in regards to the question.

The Ogham Alphabet

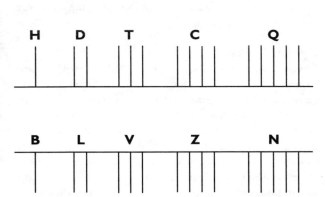

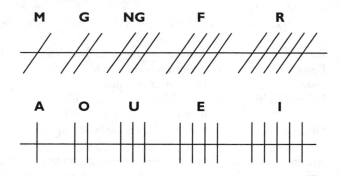

FEATHER AUGURY

Feather augury is a branch of the ancient Druid art of bird divination, which is the practice of divining the future by watching bird signs: the direction birds fly, the number of birds in a grouping, bird song, and the color and species of the birds in the group. The Celts used bird signs to forecast battles, romance, weather, and seasons.

Augury by feathers is a reminder of this ancient art of prophesy, used primarily to send secret messages to friends and lovers. The idea of feather augury is simple. For example, it is customary to send a blue and white blue jay or bluebird feather to someone you love or a red cardinal's feather to a special someone whom you wish good luck. Feathers you find point to influencing factors in your immediate future. Following is a list of feather colors and divination meanings for your reference

Feather Color   **Divination Meaning**
Green . . . . Growth, adventure, new projects,
                          prosperity

Red . . . . Reward, good luck, fortunate
opportunity
Rose . . . . A love affair, romance, heart's desire
Purple . . . . A journey or trip, nobility, balance
Blue . . . . Love, kinship, a gift
Yellow/Gold . . . . . . Friendship, companionship,
fellowship
Orange . . . . Happiness to come, new opportu-
nities, healing
Brown . . . . Good health, mastering the elements
Gray . . . . Peace of mind, tranquillity, meditation
White . . . . Pureness, gladness, joy, a birth
Blue and White . . . . A new love and/or partnership
Brown and White . . Health and happiness
Gray and White . . . . Out with the old, on with the new
Black and White . . . Beware, take care!
Black . . . . Misfortune, bad luck, transforma-
tion, death
Yellow and Green . . Gossip, back-stabbing, lies, and
small talk
Speckled/Spotted . . Divine guidance, star wisdom

TAROT

Tarot is a symbol-concept language that taps into the right
(creative) side of the brain and connects you with the archetypes of the collective unconscious. Tarot, the language of
the soul, represents a living pattern of ancient visual symbols. The Tarot, an ancient form of fortune-telling and divination, consists of seventy-eight cards—twenty-two major
arcana and fifty-six minor arcana. Its origins are disputed.
Some say the Tarot originated in Egypt and was imported

to the West by the Gypsies. Others claim the source of the Tarot is China.

Tarot can be viewed from a magical or psychological, as well as from a mythological and cultural, perspective. An excellent instructive tool, Tarot responds uniquely to each person, never teaching more than you are capable of learning.

The Druids used Tarot as a mirror and a tool for inner guidance. Each of the symbols and groups of symbols within the Tarot cards is associated with one of the four elements—air, fire, water, and earth—and corresponds to something elemental within the practitioner.

Tarot is separated into four suits, which represent the four directions and elements. The practitioner acts as the fifth element. The suits are Pentacles (diamonds), Wands (clubs), Swords (spades), and Cups (hearts). The basic qualities of each of the traditional Tarot suits in magical transformation follow.

Pentacles (Discs): Earth/North

Key Words: Abundance, money, fortune-making, trade, industry
Symbol of magical arts, the Five-pointed star, the Five senses of humankind, the Five elements of nature, the Five extremities of the body. Earth is the element of artists and craftspersons, fortune, enterprise, material well-being, comfort, and plenty.

Wands (Rods): Air/East

Key Words: Animation, energy, enterprise, growth, creativity
Air is the element of renewal, enterprise, growth, courage, and hopefulness. This element represents a world of ideas and communication.

Swords: Fire/South

Key Words: Intelligence, boldness, daring, action, transformation
Fire is the element of transformation and metamorphosis; courage in the face of danger, battle, misfortune, ruin; creativity and rebirth. Associated with intelligence, boldness, and aggression.

Cups: Water/West

Key Words: Love, balance, happiness, emotions, sensitivity
Water is the element of beauty, fertility, the subconscious mind, as well as instinct and pleasure. Strong emotions of love dwell in deep water.

Several readily available resource books explain Tarot spreads. The Celtic Cross and Tree of Life layouts are the most common spreads. One of the simplest Tarot spreads is the Threefold Spread. First, think of a question, mixing the cards in both hands. Then, draw three cards out of the deck without looking. These three cards represent the past, present, and future influences, in regards to your question.

Using the Tarot for divination involves paying close attention to symbols, numbers, and names of the cards. Note the colors used in the card and where they are placed. Look to see where the prime symbol in the card is positioned and then notice the position of all the other symbols in relation to the prime symbol. What is the prime symbol in the card doing—sitting, standing, laying down, walking, or riding? Look for any hidden or subtle symbols. What kind of vegetation, landscape, type and color of flower or facial expression is depicted? Begin to notice when a symbol occurs several times in a card. For example, how many stars are shown, or how many birds or trees? Keep in mind, numbers are also symbols in their own right.

In addition to the numbers and kinds of symbols, be aware of any geometrical symbols and where they are located on the card. How are circles, crosses, triangles, squares, or spirals used and to what effect? Merge with the symbols of the Tarot to gain a sense of the emotional content of each card. Notice the contrasting cards in the deck, for example, The Sun card and The Tower. Look at the quality of each card and begin to use metaphors for the symbols and images you see, e.g., crossing bridges, turning your back, juggling life, or charging ahead.

THE RUNES

Developed as early as 200 B.C. and introduced most probably by the Teutones and Cimbri when they invaded the Italian peninsula, rune systems have three major functions: as alphabets, for divination, and for magic. Runes were threefold symbols (form, idea, and number) that had religious and magical significance to the Celts and to all peoples who inscribed and used them. They were considered living symbols. The Elder Futhark (twenty-four runes) were used primarily until A.D. 800. Other, later rune systems were modifications of the Elder Futhark; they include the Younger (Norse) Futhark (sixteen runes) and the Anglo-Saxon Futhark (thirty-three runes).

Runes were used as a form of writing through the tenth century and as house markers to designate property through the eighteenth century. Runes were carved mostly on wood, but also on stone, metal, and bone. When carved with knife points or sharp, pointed tools dedicated and consecrated to the runic art, they were used for talismans, on grave markers, for magical binding, for decorative and symbolic art, for architecture, hex signs, and monograms.

The primal snowflake pattern, called the six-fold "Heagl," acts as the Rune Mother. When you place this rune within a solid figure, every runic form can be derived from it because of its numerical shape and value. One modern-day symbol, the peace sign, is a derivative of the Yr-rune of the Younger Futhark.

To use runes for divination, first either make or purchase a set of runes. You can make a set easily from wood, stones, or clay. Making your own runes fills them with your personal energy and power, like a signature. Carve the runic symbols and paint them in gold or red. Keep your runes in a wide-mouthed rune bag, which is ideal for putting your hand into to pull out the runes one by one.

Begin by asking a specific question before drawing out or casting your runes. The Three Rune Layout is easy to do; it represents influences on the question or issue at hand. The first rune symbolizes the beginning, the second rune the middle, and the third rune the end, or outcome, of the particular issue.

For example, recently I had a question about my relationship with my son. I pulled three runes—the S, TH, and W. The S rune represented my success in having a son and the sunshine he has given me in my life. The TH rune stood for my son's strong will and his current streak of independent action and thought. The W rune represented the future, indicating my relationship with my son would be filled with joy, fellowship, and goodwill.

Another way to use runes for divination is to open your rune bag, and while asking the question, stir the runes up with your hand without looking at them. Then cast the entire contents of the bag out on a white cloth. The cloth usually has symbols on it, designating the past, present, and future, and the four elemental points of North, East, South and West. The answer to your question is then determined by the positions of the runes as they fall on the cloth.

Rune Symbols and Meanings

ᚠ	A	os	Ancestral God; the rune of poetry, song, writing, speech, and magical incantation.
ᛒ	B	beorc	Birch Goddess, Earth Mother; the Threefold cycle of birth, life, and death; oneness and protection.
ᛞ	D	daeg	Day, the balance between night and day, polarity; rune of sunrise, sunset, dawn, and twilight.
ᛖ	E	eoh	Horse, stallion, the power of the twin Gods; travel to Otherworlds; prophecy, trust, loyalty, and marriage.
ᚠ	F	feh	Mobile property, money; rules the basic force of fertility.
ᚷ	G	geofu	Gifts of the Goddess and God, the giver and the given; the rune of female/male polarities.
ᚻ	H	heagl	Hail, cosmic seed and primordial pattern; Rune Mother; union and evolution within a fixed framework.
ᛁ	I	is	Ice, primal matter/antimatter; the forces of creation, concentration, and ego integration and balance.
ᛃ	J	gear:	Year, harvest, the solar year cycle, fertility, reward, and luck.

Rune	Letter	Name	Meaning
<	K	can	Torch, internal and controlled fire; rune of the artist, craftsperson, and creativity.
↑	L	lagu:	Water, sea, the wave; source of organic life, second sight, magnetism, and initiation.
M	M	man:	Human being, divine link, sacred marriage of the Earth Mother and Sky Father; rune of memory and mental power.
N	N	nied	Need, need-fire; necessity, resistance, and deliverance from distress.
◇	O	eoel	Inheritance, noble, immobile ancestral property, homeland; inherited power, wealth, prosperity, and family.
P	P	peod	Dance (of fate), perception, divination, change; the rune of time.
R	R	radh	Solar wagon, chariot, universal rhythm; rune of ritual and natural law.
S	S	sygil	Sun (feminine), the solar wheel, spiritual will, victory, success, and guidance.
↑	T	tir	Honor, war, judgment by arms, law, justice, world order, and spiritual discipline.
∩	U	ur	Aurock, Bison, Ox, the primal forming force, the cosmic seed.
P	W	wynn	Joy, pleasure, delight from a common source; fellowship, goodwill, and binding energy.

Rune	Name	Meaning
▷	TH thorn	Thorn, the strong one, directed cosmic force of defense and destruction, instinctual will.
◇	NG ing	Hero, Earth God, storehouse of potential energy, gestation, fertility, and sexuality.
Ψ	Final eolhs Z or R	Elk, Swan, protection, defense, victory; rune of the spirit.

The Celtic
Resurgence Today

Currently, Celtic spirituality and tradition are once again coming to the forefront. In the last century, the Celtic myths and legends have begun to exist alongside the classical Greek and Roman myths, which once dominated European literature.

Opportunities to study and practice the Earth-centered traditions of Celtic spirituality are growing. Groups teaching Celtic spirituality include the Druids, the Faery, and Wicca. Several books on the subject have been published, many with practical information you can try on your own. Celtic music has filtered into the mainstream and continues to gain popularity. Films with Celtic themes are extremely popular. Numerous Web sites on the Internet provide listings of Celtic groups and publications.

It is important to remember that the wisdom of the Celtic peoples, especially the Druids, was developed over many thousands of years and represents several interlinked traditions passed down from ancestral times. Studying and practicing the older traditions has a very real effect on our consciousness; a slow and mysterious change occurs within our very spirit.

Many people are beginning to hear the call of the Goddess, connecting with the sacred spirit of the land in a way similar to the ancient Celts. In the past, humankind has collectively rejected and destroyed the ever-present paradise. We must learn to seek it once again, find it, and realize it. Connecting with the divine light of the Goddess and God, indeed with the sacred Earth Light that sleeps within the land, is one profound way to do this.

Humanity and the land are inseparable aspects of fluid reality, a fluid, or protean world that transforms and regenerates itself. Living power traditions such as Celtic spirituality show us how to enter the infinite realms of inspiration, creativity, and potential. We are the ancestors of future wisdom and generations. Joining together, we can be the redeemers, restorers, and regenerators of the Fallen Land. Now is the time to bring the light back to the dark land.

Glossary

All Father: The consort and father.

All Mother: The Goddess and mother.

Amulet: An object traditionally made of metal or stone that has feelings or effects placed in it. Often carried on the person either as a ring or necklace.

Archetypes: Symbolic representations of universal principles, defining concepts in a symbolic form.

Athame: A ceremonial knife, two-sided, representing the element fire.

Avalon: Land of the Otherworld, apple land, a harmonic of energy in oneness.

Beltane: Fourth Great Day at the beginning of May. Also known as Bel Fire (Bel meaning bright) and The Adventure of the Sun.

Bowl: Craft tool used for salt or water.

Bridget's Fire: The second Great Day following Yule.

Bright One: The Bright aspects of the All Mother, representing light and the living.

Candle: Represents the fire element in magical works.

Candlestick(s): Craft tool(s) used on the altar. Customarily three candlesticks with three candles (green—left side of altar, red—right side of altar, white—at the center).

Celts: The ancient Gauls and Britons. Welsh, Irish, Highland Scot, Manx, Cornish, and Breton peoples of central and western Europe.

Chalice: A loving cup traditionally made of metal or clay. A consecrated tool symbolizing the water element and the concept of oneness.

Circle: Sacred light space constructed by the practitioner for magical work. Also refers to the Family of the Tuatha.

Concept of Oneness: Foundation of Druid tradition, saying that all things are one whatsoever they may be.

Consort: Mate and lover of a divine being.

Craft Tools: Athame, Chalice, Wand, Robe, Cord, Incense Burner, Candlestick, and Bowl. Consecrated instruments used to aid the practitioner in merging.

Dark One: The Dark aspect of the All Mother who represents death and rebirth.

Days of Power: The eight Great Days and thirteen High Moons of ritual celebration.

Divination: The art and science of forecasting or reading events using traditional tools such as oghams, runes, and tarot cards.

Dragon Veins: The visible energy that is generated by ley lines.

Eight-Spoked Wheel: The wheel of the sun, which includes the eight Great Days. Each spoke denotes one of these days.

Elements: Four traditional elements, often a fifth. Fire, earth, air, and water. The fifth element is the practitioner or spirit.

Fabric of Life: The endless Celtic weave representing the totality of all manifest reality.

Faery: Beings within the land that are one step away in awareness from our "waking" reality. The Tuatha De Dannan who have merged with the land.

Feast: A celebration meal in honor of the Goddess and God.

Four Wards: The four corners of North, East, South, and West. Also called the Watch Towers or the Great Wards.

Four Keys: Wisdom, self-responsibility, self-honesty, and love.

God: An individual being who exists in a merged state.

Goddess: An individual being who exists in a merged state.

Godhood: The attainment of becoming a God/dess. A being who has gone through the three great merges, moving beyond time and space.

Great Book: The written rituals, oral stories, and teachings of Celtic Gwyddonic Druidism.

Great Days: The eight Great Days, the Wheel of Taranos, including the solstices, the equinoxes, and the midpoints.

Great Goddess: The term encompassing all of the faces and qualities of goddess energy.

Hellith's Day: The seventh Great Day, usually celebrating the harvest, which takes place on the Autumnal Equinox.

High Moons: The twelve or thirteen full moons in a yearly cycle. Starting with the first full moon after Yule, they are the Wolf, Storm, Chaste, Seed, Hare, Dyad, Mead, Wort, Barley, Wine, Blood, Snow, and Oak. A time of healing rituals and for dreaming.

Lady's Day: Also called Hertha's Day. The third Great Day of the cycle, traditionally associated with the beginning of Spring.

Letha's Day: The sixth Great day of the cycle, also called Midsummer.

Lughnassad: The seventh Great Day, which takes place in August. Lugh's wedding feast. Considered the time when the forces of light and dark converge, when the sun and moon are equal.

Mabinogi: Welsh Bardic tales and stories of the lives of heroines and heroes. The Four Monads.

Magic: The study of the nature of all things. The use of ritual to continue the cycle of the Goddess and God.

Merging: The state of becoming one with all things. Diffusing into the boundless.

Negativity: A destructive energetic force that breaks patterns and feeds upon itself. Moving counterclockwise pulls off energy. Associated with the Dark One.

Ninefold One: The tripled representation of the triplicity. Nine faces of the goddess in one.

Oghams: Form of symbol writing invented by the consort Ogmios.

Oneness: The boundless. A place where one is connected to all things and to nothing.

Otherworld: The dwelling place of the Goddess and God and all of the divine beings of oneness, such as the Faery. Another very "real" dimension of perception and awareness.

Patterns: A term for discussing one's intentions and expectations. The formula and foundation from which one merges with and experiences all things.

Positivity: An energetic force that creates and builds energy and patterns. Associated with the Bright One.

Practitioner: A person who practices magic.

Priest: Man representing the God or consort.

Priestess: Woman representing the Goddess.

Prophecy: Prediction under divine influence and direction. Reading patterns successfully.

Rapport: Harmony of relationship with another, to be in close accord. Remembering who we really are and understanding the deeper connection.

Robe: Your sacred and magical skin.

Sacred Marriage: Spiritual union with the Goddess and God. You become the Goddess and God.

Salt: A purifier representing the earth element.

Samhain: All Hollows Eve and the eighth Great Day, associated with death and rebirth. The day when the veil between time and space is the thinnest.

Shapeshifting: An extremely deep merge. Shifting into the double.

Solstices: Days of power in the times during summer and winter when the sun is at its greatest distance from the celestial equator.

Sunwise: Clockwise turn, which is considered the positive direction, builds energy. The opposite of widdershins or counterclockwise.

Symbols: Representation of many things in one thing.

Talisman: A item that is filled with a feeling, sensation, or attitude used for magic.

Tarot Cards: A divination tool using archetypal and symbolic visual representations.

Three Eyes of Kerridwen: The formula for magical works, consisting of expectation, desire, and merging.

Threefold One: The Triple Goddess, representing birth, life, and rebirth. Three faces of the goddess in one.

Tir na N'Og: Land of Promise and the Celtic paradise.

Tuatha De Dannan: The family of Danu, title of the gods.

Underworld: Land of the Faery.

Wand: Traditionally made of wood and decorated with stones, representing the element air.

Yule: The first of the Great Days celebrated on the Winter Solstice.

Further Reading

Arrien, Angeles. *The Tarot Handbook*. Sonoma, CA: Arcus Publishing Company, 1987.

Bonwick, James. *Irish Druids and Old Irish Religions*. New York: Dorset, 1986.

Bord, Janet and Bord, Colin. *Mysterious Britain*. London: Paladin Books, 1974.

Campbell, Joseph. *The Masks of God, Vol. I–IV*. New York: Penguin Books, 1977.

Ceram, C. W. *Gods, Graves and Scholars*. New York: Bantam Books, 1972.

Devereaux, Paul. *Secrets of Ancient and Sacred Places*. London: Blandford Press, 1992.

Eisler, Riane. *The Chalice and the Blade: Our History, Our Future*. San Francisco: Harper & Row, 1987.

Eliade, Mircea. *Shamanism*. Bollingen Series: Princeton, New Jersey, 1964.

Ford, Patrick K. (Translator). *The Mabinogi and Other Medieval Welsh Tales*. Los Angeles: University of California Press, 1977.

Frazier, Sir James George. *The Golden Bough*. New York: The Macmillan Company, 1935.

Gimbutas, Marija. *The Goddesses and Gods of Old Europe*. Berkeley, CA: University of California Press, 1982.

Gimbutas, Marija. *The Language of the Goddess*. San Francisco: Harper & Row, 1989.

Graves, Robert. *The White Goddess*. New York: Faber & Faber, 1966.

Grimal, Pierre (Ed.). *Larousse World Mythology*. London: Paul Hamlyn, 1965.

King, John. *The Celtic Druids' Year*. London: Blandford, 1994.

Knight, Gareth. *The Secret Tradition in Arthurian Legend*. York Beach, MA: Samuel Weiser, Inc., 1996.

Knight, Sirona. *Greenfire: Making Love with the Goddess*. St. Paul, MN: Llewellyn Publications, 1995.

Knight, Sirona. *Moonflower: Erotic Dreaming with the Goddess*. St. Paul, MN: Llewellyn Publications, 1996.

Leach, Maria (Ed.). *Standard Dictionary of Folklore, Mythology, and Legend*. New York: Funk & Wagnalls Co., 1950.

Markale, Jean. *Merlin: Priest of Nature*. Rochester, VT: Inner Traditions, 1995.

Monaghan, Patricia. *The Book of Goddesses and Heroines*. St. Paul, MN: Llewellyn Publications, 1990.

Mormouth, Geoffrey. *History of the Kings of Britain*. New York: E.P. Dutton & Co., 1958.

Murray, Margaret. *The God of the Witches*. London: Oxford University Press, 1970.

Spence, Lewis. *The History and Origins of Druidism*. New York: Samuel Weiser, Inc., 1971.

Starck, Marcia. *Women's Medicine Ways*. Freedom, CA: The Crossing Press, 1994.

Stein, Diane. *The Goddess Celebrates*. Freedom, CA: The Crossing Press, 1995.

Stewart, R. J., and Williamson, Robin. *Celtic Bards, Celtic Druids*. London: Blandford Press, 1996.

Stewart, R. J., *Celtic Gods, Celtic Goddesses*. New York: Sterling Publishing Co., 1990.

Yeats, W. B. (Ed.). *Fairy & Folk Tales of Ireland*. New York: Macmillan Publishing Co., 1983.